Ancestry's JOURNEY

by Susan Davis

D1384810

SGD PUBLISHING COMPANY

Library of Congress Catalog Card Number: 2013901600

ISBN: 978-0-615-75609-7

Printed in the United States of America by Mennonite Press, Inc.,
Newton, KS

Dedication

In memory of my ancestors who endured countless hardships with courage, strength and humility through the eyes of faith. What a beautiful example they left behind for future generations to follow. I'm honored to be a part of their family tree.

Special thanks to my husband Ben, my mom Florence and my daughter Sarah for their contributions to, "Ancestry's Journey." Each of you lightened my journey in writing this book.

Introduction

Ancestries are as numerous as the stars of a clear night sky. Every family has a different combination. Like clockwork, nights turn to days and days back to nights, years fly by and the link to ones forerunners may seem as far away as the stars.

Perhaps that is why the earlier period of time is intriguing to many. They have a glimmer of hope that if they learn more about the roots of their family tree they will feel more whole. So they embark on a mission to find out all they can about the relatives who preceded themselves.

"Ancestry's Journey" is based upon known facts about my family tree as much as possible. I also did some research to fill in many blank spaces. The rest is purely a weaving together of a story of what life might have been like for my ancestors in Russia beginning in 1911.

Fortunately, I knew each of my grandparents and their personalities in the later years of their lives. I did my best to incorporate those characteristic traits into who they were at a much younger age.

In Russia and in America, farm life was a huge part of my ancestors' lives. On the small farm where I grew up, I learned firsthand about some of the same work they did in sugar beet fields and milking cows by hand. In other ways, I experienced a more modern way of farming.

While growing up, my mom cooked a few German-Russian foods, and she called them by their German names. Glace was one of the main dishes she made. On occasion, she baked apple strudel or fried grebble for desserts. Naturally, she learned how to prepare those ethnic foods and others from her mother. Since American food was served at our family table most of the time, some foods she grew up eating were forgotten about and are now lost forever.

As a teenager, it wasn't uncommon for my aging grandparents to speak in German to my parents. Most of the time, they did this for a good reason. They didn't want my siblings and me to understand what they were talking about.

Recently, I found it intriguing and puzzling when Mom told me, "My parents and grandparents didn't talk about life in Russia. I've heard other people say the same thing." Maybe it was because life was hard, and the memories they had were scarred with more pain than happiness. America was the right answer for them. The country gave them freedom and the opportunity to build new lives.

While writing "Ancestry's Journey", I was able to sprinkle a few German words throughout the book. Other than that, it is written solely in English – the language my immigrant ancestors were forced to learn if they wanted to survive in America. In the process, the native German they grew up knowing slowly slipped away, beyond the horizon.

My first published book, "Small Farm & Big Family" was about growing up on a small farm and being part of a big family. "Ancestry's Journey" takes readers further back into my family history by two generations. It leads them down a path to present day to where my ancestors' legacy has guided me. You'll discover what they left behind.

A German-Russian descendant – forever...
by Susan Davis

Contents

1
Family Trees

On a quiet afternoon, Susan (better known by her relatives as Suz) sat at her dining room table, pondering over bits and pieces of family history. The few pictures she had collected were but a glimmer of time in the lives of her ancestors. She had also accumulated a small number of documents, which in their day had served in an official capacity. With the passage of years, they'd also become historical family documents.

As she studied the tidbits of information, Suz found new questions arose. It was as if she were putting together a large jigsaw puzzle without a picture to guide her. It was also like looking at a huge, old tree that had a gnarly, weathered trunk. Some of the branches had remained intact, but others had broken off during storms and had come crashing down to the ground. It wasn't as simple as gluing them back into place. Each splinter had to line up perfectly for the tree to regain its skeleton form. The majority of everyday facts about her family history had been blown away like fragile leaves and were now lost forever. She was well aware of the fact that one erroneous turn would lead her down a wrong path.

Suz felt grateful, luckier than many, that she had a firm foundation to work from. She knew it was a fact that all of her great grandparents had been born in the Volga River Region of Russia and had immigrated to the United States between the years of 1911 to 1913. Their predecessors had left Germany sometime after 1763 when Catherine the Great was appealing for foreigners to settle in Russia. Her manifesto promised them free land, a 30-year tax exemption, religious freedom, self- government and a permanent exemption from military service. At the time, Europe was dealing with poverty and the Seven Years War was about to draw to a close. Catherine the Great's deal enticed many Germans to leave their homeland, including all of my ancestors.

It was great that Suz had names and dates to work with, but that wasn't what she really was searching for. She wished she could have personally known her great grandparents and the generations who came before them. What circumstances molded their lives? Did she share some of their personality traits? Why did her great grandparents cling to their German ancestry even though their family had been in Russia for nearly 150 years? Were they frightened, excited or both as they left Russia, crossed an ocean and entered a new land? Did they miss the Old World? What became of the older relatives, who were unable to make the journey to America? Questions – Suz had many things she wanted to inquire about, but were the answers located anywhere?

When she heard the front door of the house open, she was instantly transported back to the present. Her husband Ben was home from work. "Whatcha' doin'?" he asked, standing behind her and peering over her right shoulder.

"Looking over family history," she replied. She began

picking up the strewn papers, placing them back into the ring binder where she kept them. Her quiet concentration time was over. There was no way she was going to make any progress now. The project she had been working on was confusing enough without any distractions.

Invariably, whenever Ben knew she was searching for another piece of her roots, his thoughts would turn to his own family history. "At least you know what country all of your relatives came from and when they did. I don't know that much. For all I know, some of them might have come over on the Mayflower," he remarked. "I'm like a mutt. I probably have a little of this blood and a little of that."

What he said was true. Suz couldn't argue with that, but they both knew some interesting facts about one side of his family history. His great grandparents, William and Nancy Jane Oshel, traveled by covered wagon across Kansas from Olathe to Medicine Lodge in 1890. His redheaded grandmother Bertha was seven-years-old on that trip. As the covered wagon trekked its way over the prairie, she had a lot in common with Laura Ingalls Wilder. More than likely, she could have easily related to the book, "Little House on the Prairie."

While Laura had her share of adventures, Bertha got to experience something the famous writer never did. The historic day was September 16, 1893, and the Cherokee Strip in Oklahoma was about to be opened for settlement. The Oshel family was lined up on the Kansas border along with approximately 100,000 other people. Her father was hoping to claim a quarter section (160 acres) of land. The strip, which was previously inhabited by Indians, was 50 miles wide by 200 miles long.

As William waited on the line, he was wearing a flaming red shirt and was mounted on a huge, white stallion. He dressed this way so that his family would be able to easily find him. His wife and children were in their wagon, and his brother Bruce was at the reins. They would follow behind to the previously selected site.

When the gun sounded, William and other prospective landowners were off in a chaotic flash, kicking up plenty of dust. While crossing Mule Creek, the wagon became stuck. In their attempt to free it, they spilled a great deal of their precious water supply. It was a trying day for them, but toward evening they were grateful to find William. He was ecstatic, because he had staked the claim he wanted.

The next morning, William discovered a squatter was camped out on the section that he had rightfully claimed. "You're trespassing!" he shouted. "I drove in my marker before you did!" A gunfight was about to take place when another man came riding up on horseback. He informed them that homesteading wasn't for him, and he was willing to sell the claim he staked for five dollars. It was only a few miles away. Being a family man, William made a wise choice. He paid the rider and moved his wife and children to the other location near Alva, Oklahoma.

Thus began hard days of pioneering for the Oshels. In order to farm the land, they first had to break up the sod with workhorses and a plow. While many of the pioneers got discouraged and moved away, William and Nancy Jane did not quit. They persisted through the lean times and eventually prospered.

The opening of the Cherokee Strip was Oklahoma's largest land rush, and it made the history books. Bertha no doubt would have had vivid memories of the once in a lifetime event, plus many others of their homesteading days. "You should have paid attention to the stories your grandmother told," Suz chided her husband.

"Back then, I wasn't interested in hearing those old stories," he admitted readily. "They were boring!"

Suz knew Ben well enough that she could picture him toning out a family discussion about days gone by. For him, it was as easy as turning the volume of a radio down so he didn't have to listen to it. "I do remember Grandma saying that they first lived in a dugout, and they ate prairie dogs to survive."

"How long did they live in the dugout?"

"I'm not sure," he answered. "Mom told me that my great grandfather built a really nice three-story house, which had a basement. A tornado destroyed it and the rest of their outbuildings around 1908. She remembered that her grandpa and three uncles rebuilt their property."

"Can you imagine how much work that would be?"

"My great grandfather must have been a good carpenter," Ben reasoned. "You've got to know what you're doing when you build a house." There was a pause in the conversation before he changed the subject. "I also remember Grandma talking about all the rattlesnakes there were. She ran barefooted across the prairie and so did her sisters and brothers. The snakes never even slowed them down. They just jumped over them and kept on going."

"I was ornery when I was a kid, but I can't picture myself doing that," Suz grimaced. "They could have been struck so easily and medical help wasn't readily available. It would have been tough to settle in a new territory. Your ancestors had to be strong."

The stories Ben regrets not paying attention to are now truly gone. Years ago, Suz had read all of Bertha's diaries that she began keeping in the mid 1940s. She was hoping there would be some interesting old stories recorded there, but they were missing on her penned pages. Instead, she wrote about everyday events like the weather, what she was sewing on, who they visited with, the price they had paid for merchandise, the gardens and chickens she raised, etc. Her feelings were never expressed in the journals.

One thing Suz and Ben know for sure is that his ancestors' participation in the Oklahoma Land Rush is still positively affecting their family today. They were taken by surprise when an oil company contacted them about an oil and gas lease on William and Nancy Jane's homestead. The land has since been sold, but the family wisely held onto the mineral rights.

"You complain that you don't know much about your family history," Suz commented, "but the mineral rights you inherited are a direct tie to your ancestors. Considering they homesteaded there 120 years ago, that's pretty amazing."

Ben thought for a moment before agreeing, "You're right. It's something in my family that has been passed down from generation to generation."

2
Cold Russians

In October 1962, Suz was a nine-year-old fourth grader at a country school in northeastern Colorado. She was having a hard time paying attention to her teacher, because she was worried. She'd heard on the news that there was a Cuban Missile Crisis. Russia was threatening to launch nuclear weapons toward the United States at any moment, and she took their threat seriously. It was reported that the missiles had the capability of reaching nearly every state in the nation and cause mass destruction. She was certain that Colorado would be one of the targets. Instead of concentrating on her assignment like she should have been, she was staring out of the large classroom window. She thought it might be possible to see a missile coming. Maybe then she would have time to hide under her desk, and the bomb wouldn't hurt her.

Then Suz's imagination swung into full gear, and she could picture the peacefulness of the plains being shattered. Missiles would come speeding in like a monstrous storm. There would be devastation everywhere, and the

United States would have no choice but to fire back. Perhaps a nuclear war would destroy all life. If people survived the attack, radiation could make everyone terribly sick.

Even though Suz was a young girl, she could tell that Russians were not well liked by Americans. In fact, they were almost hated. She wasn't the only one who feared them; adults did, too. She'd heard some people had even constructed bomb shelters. It was confusing to her, because she knew all of her grandparents were German-Russians. They certainly were very nice people. They were honest, hard-working Americans, who would never cause trouble for anyone. Maybe that's why they had to leave Russia.

Fortunately, President Kennedy managed to get the intense crisis back under control, but the Cold War continued to simmer. Communism was a persistent threat.

When Suz wasn't at school, she was at home on the small farm where she lived with her large family. It was a peaceful place to be. It felt like a world away from Russia and communism, so why be anxious about it any longer? She put the matter out of her mind and enjoyed being a kid.

Even when Suz became an adult, Russia still seemed a world away. She'd never been there for a visit, but she was certainly intrigued with the faraway country where her ancestors had lived. So when Sam, a member of her church, told her his lineage went back to Russia, she felt an immediate connection. "My grandfather was a good storyteller," he commented. "He told me an interesting story about his father going into town during the winter for supplies. I don't know if it's true or not, but here's what he told me. Four or five men always made the hazardous trip together. Three horses were used to pull the sled. The driver handled them, while the other men were equipped with black snake whips. Wild, hungry wolves would undoubtedly be out on the prowl, searching for an easy meal. The horses' weight caused them to sink into the deep snow, but the predators were light enough they could run on the hard crust. Therefore, the horses were at a big disadvantage. The anxious men were constantly surveying the countryside looking for the predators. They knew a lead wolf would come in first followed by the pack. They became experts at snapping their whips and killing them."

"No wonder a group of men went into town together!" Suz exclaimed. She could picture the horrific scene in her mind.

"They had to for protection," Sam stated matter-of-factly. "A pack of wolves could easily kill the horses or the men."

While their whips protected them from the wolves, being bundled up in warm, heavy clothing sheltered them from the bitter winter weather. Suz had seen stern-looking Russians on TV wearing Ushanka hats. Their fur caps had ear flaps that could be tied under their chins or up on the crown of their hats. She'd also seen her grandpa wear this type of hat in winter. When he did so, he looked very much like a Russian. It stood to reason for he had been born in that country and lived the first 15 years of his life there. She smiled as she recalled how as an elderly man he had slowly driven his older car along the streets of Sterling, Colorado. He was short in stature and could barely see over the steering wheel. When other drivers glanced over at him, the first thing they saw was his Russian hat.

Sam regained Suz's attention when he said, "Years later when my great grandparents immigrated to America, they brought five cans of wheat with them. It was stored in one of their trunks. During their journey, they stayed near their belongings so their possessions wouldn't get stolen. The contents in those trunks were priceless to them. That's all they owned."

He went on to explain how his ancestors had settled in

Kansas. "The first year my great grandmother wanted my great grandfather to plant all of the wheat. He didn't listen to her and only planted two cans of seed. He stored the rest for future use. It was a good thing he did, because their first crop was poor because of drought."

"He made a wise choice," Suz commented. "When you don't have much, you have to be very careful with how you use it."

The story got Suz to thinking about her ancestors. They were all farmers, but they had grown very little wheat. The main crops they raised were sugar beets, corn, hay and oats. She doubted they would have brought any hard winter wheat seed over from Russia. The Mennonites had been credited with boosting Kansas's wheat production by planting the Turkey Red variety. All of her great grandparents were Catholic.

She began to wonder if her relatives had squirreled away some other kind of seeds and transported them across the ocean to the new land. Garden seeds...they could have easily brought some of them.

Suz recalled the big gardens she helped her family raise. On several occasions, she remembered her mom taking a bite of juicy cantaloupe and commenting, "This is a really good one. I'm going to keep these seeds for next year." She knew her mother's routine. She'd rinse them off, wrap them up in a rag, tie it shut with an old string and hang it out on the clothesline to dry.

In the spring of the year, Mom soaked the pouch filled with cantaloupe seeds in water to soften them. This helped them to sprout quicker. By being frugal, she saved money and was able to plant quality seeds. It certainly seemed like an old-fashioned custom. Suz speculated that she had learned this technique from her parents, and they picked it up from theirs.

She recalled her father explaining why his grandparents had settled in northeastern Colorado. The land and the weather were similar to the Volga River Region where they had farmed in Russia. So it would stand to reason that any seeds they brought with them would have thrived in the new climate.

3
Anna
Suz's grandmother on her father's side

As surely as the wind of time blows through the ages, so shall generations come and go. Some generations stay put exactly where they are planted, whereas others must step out on a limb and pave a new way for those to come.
The journey begins in 1911.

O n the hilly side of the Volga River in Russia, the simple village of Volmer was established by German immigrants in 1766. The colony was named after its first mayor. All of the residents spoke Low German and were devout Catholics. A church, rectory and a schoolhouse were built at the center of their settlement. The teacher was responsible for instructing the children in religion, reading and writing.

In 1871, Czar Alexander II, great grandson of Catherine the Great, began revoking the privileges that the empress had granted the immigrants in her manifesto. German-

13

Russian villages all along the Volga River were affected. The government began treating them like peasants. In an effort to "Russianize" them, schools were placed in government control. The authorities also changed Volmer's name to Kopenka, but the stubborn settlers didn't adopt it. They continued calling it by its original name.

By 1874, young German-Russian men were being drafted into the military, having to serve six-year terms. Two years later, it was ruled that the immigrants could no longer have their own courts and judges. Russian judges were appointed, and crimes committed by the Russian people against the villagers didn't get punished fairly. This was a troubling situation for them.

In the summer of 1911, Anna Ertle was one of those who lived in Volmer. She was nine-years-old, old enough to understand the safest place she could be was within the boundaries of the village. Papa and Mama had made that clear.

The young girl with light brown hair and blue eyes wasn't burdened by adult troubles. The beautiful weather made her feel carefree and happy as she ran and played with other children her age. She did miss her father who had left quite a while back to travel to America. Papa had gone there in search of a new home for them. She had often heard the adults call America, "The Golden Land." From that description, it sounded like a beautiful country to her.

Meanwhile, Mama took care of Anna and her five younger siblings. They eagerly waited for word from him. Day after day, they never received a letter. One night, while they were eating supper, Anna saw her mother get a faraway look in her gray eyes before saying, "I wish we would hear from your father." She sighed before adding, "I hope nothing has happened to him."

"Papa's fine," Anna tried to reassure her mother. "It probably takes the mail a long time to travel that far."

"It most certainly does," Mama agreed before giving her a gentle hug.

Once word did arrive, Anna knew it would mean one of two things for her family. Papa had not found what he was searching for in America, and he was on his way home; or they would be packing up their meager belongings and traveling to a foreign country to start a brand new life. She wondered if they would be better off staying right where they were. What she had overheard adults saying was true—the Russians weren't overly friendly to them. Still, there were lots of other families living in Volmer in the same shoes as they were in. They had become a close knit community, because they had to.

She liked her neighbors from across the street. Their last name was Gartner. They had a bunch of kids to play with. Johannes was their second oldest son. He was fourteen-years-old so he didn't play with them. She had noticed that he kept busy helping his father with their horses and farming, and it showed. Although he was short, he was very strong for his age. Little did she know in 1911 just how important he would become in her life.

One afternoon when Anna's mother, her sisters and brother went to visit a widow lady, she stayed at home by herself. She'd rather do that than sit and listen to Mama and the older woman talking.

Anna hadn't planned on being nosy, but she had always wanted to look inside Papa's special book. She now had the perfect opportunity to do so. He had strictly instructed her and the rest of her siblings to never touch it, but she couldn't stand it any longer. Her imagination was telling her it might contain some secret information. Her hands were trembling as she carefully got it out and opened it

15

up. She was afraid that her family might come home unex-
pectedly, and she'd get caught. It felt wrong to disobey her
father, but he was a world away. He couldn't scold her now.
She even thought the book might have some pretty pictures in it, but there were none. Only the first few pages
were written on; the rest of them were blank. Her father's
penmanship wasn't very good, but she was able to make
out what was written. He had scribbled down the day he
had married her mother. Below it was a list of birth dates
of everyone in her family. Under them was a record of their
baptisms and their sponsors. Anna knew it was important
information and should never be lost. Her curiosity had
been fulfilled. She quickly put the important book back
where it belonged.

An instant later, a knock on the front door startled her.
She was afraid to answer it, not knowing who was on the
other side. So she opened it just a crack and peeked out.
The first thing she saw was a pair of work worn hands.
They were holding a letter. Her eyes then traveled up to the
man's sunburned face. It was Joseph Gartner, their neighbor, and his son Johannes. She opened the door the rest
of the way. "Anna, I just got back from Saratov. That city
is too big for me – too many people living there for my
liking. The reason I stopped by is I picked up the village's
mail, and this letter was addressed to your mother. It looks
important, like it might be from your father. Make sure you
give it to her," he instructed.

"Thank you," Anna said, taking it from him. She glanced
down at the writing on the outside of the envelope, and it
matched the handwriting she had just seen in the special
book. It was indeed from Papa. She looked up and smiled
gratefully before saying, "Mama has been waiting every
day for it."

"I imagine she has been," her neighbor agreed, smiling

down at her. He then looked at his son and added, "We've got plenty of farm work to do, and it isn't getting done like this." She watched them walk briskly away.

Anna immediately realized what she must do. She clutched the precious letter in her right hand and raced across the dirt streets of Volmer. She knew exactly where her mother's friend lived. Mama would be glad that she ran the letter over to her as soon as she got it. She was out of breath by the time she knocked on the front door. The widow was old, and it took her a while to open the door. "Do come in," she said in a welcoming manner.

Typically, Anna would kindly ask the old lady how she was doing but not today. She was too excited for friendly talk. She quickly blurted out, "I need to show Mama the letter that just came!"

Within seconds, her mother appeared in the doorway. She quickly tore the envelope open, unfolded the letter and read in silence. After what seemed like an eternity, she looked at the older woman and revealed what it had said. "John told me to get our passports and shots in order. We are to get on the first ship that we can and head for America. He has settled in Iliff, Colorado, and he thinks we will have a much better life there."

"You're not going to be traveling alone with six young children, are you?"

"I'll help take care of my sisters and brother," Anna volunteered wholeheartedly.

"She's a very good helper," Mama replied. "John says it doesn't make sense for him to travel back to Russia. It would cost too much, and we don't have any extra money to spend on that trip."

"People around the village will certainly pitch in and help with the packing," the widow said. "It's the long journey across the ocean that I'm concerned about."

17

"I'll ask around. Surely another family will be leaving on the same ship we do," Anna's mother assured her. "We'll miss everyone here, but I do think it is best for us to make the big move. We got plenty of things to do now so we should go home and get busy."

Anna could tell the letter had given Mama a new bounce in her step. As they made their way along the dirt streets of the village, she occasionally had to run just to keep up with her. "When will we be leaving?" she asked.

"Just as soon as I can get the arrangements made, but that's going to take some time," Mama replied.

"Oh," Anna said softly as they stepped back into their simple house. Suddenly she realized that she would be leaving the only home she had known since her birth. Once they set sail for America, she had no expectations of ever returning. A few tears came to her eyes. She would be saying goodbye to her friends. It almost didn't seem fair to have to make such a drastic choice; but, of course, that decision didn't lie on her small shoulders. It belonged to her parents, and they had already made their decision. Her mind felt like a blur. Everything was happening too quickly.

4
Saving Seeds

It was the end of August, and it was a beautiful morning. The sun was shining brightly through the deep blue sky. Anna, her sister Myrtle and brother Joseph were out in their big garden picking schwartzbeeren (German word for blackberries.) The round berries had ripened to a dark purple and were now turning black. Their smooth skins had changed from shiny to dull. The bushes, which were about two feet tall, were loaded with clusters of pea-size berries. Anna tossed a few in her mouth. The flavorful blackberries popped open and a multitude of tiny seeds burst forth. The fruit wasn't sweet, but it wasn't bitter either. It was somewhere in between. Mama would add some sugar when she cooked them.

Anna had grown up eating the blackberries, and she loved them. All of the villagers grew them in their gardens and cooked lots of delicious foods with them. They were a part of their culture.

"How many more do we have to pick?" Myrtle asked, interrupting her oldest sister's thoughts.

"We've barely got started," Anna replied. "Mama told me she wants to make strudel and that takes a lot of berries. She also wants us to pick some extra ones. She's going to dry a bunch of seeds and save them, just like she did with the other garden seeds. Remember when she cut up scraps of cloth and filled them with the dried seeds and tied the pouches shut. We're taking blackberry, watermelon, cantaloupe, cucumber and dill seeds with us when we go to America."

"Why are we doing that?" five-year-old Joseph joined in on the conversation.

"We're going to plant them," Anna answered. "Mama told me that Papa's letter said that he didn't see any blackberries growing in that country. So if we want to raise them, we've got to take seed with us."

"Do you think we'll have a big garden?" Myrtle asked.

"Hope so," Anna replied. "Mama says as long as we can grow our own food we'll never go hungry."

"I don't like being hungry!" Joseph exclaimed just before he stuffed a handful of ripe berries into his waiting mouth.

Anna could tell that Joseph wasn't going to be much help with the picking; but, at least, he was having fun out in the garden. She didn't mind picking the ripe berries from their stems, but she did get tired of sitting on her homemade stool.

It was nearly noon when Anna, Myrtle and Joseph carried the berries into the house. "I was beginning to wonder where you were," Mama said, wiping her hands on her apron. She pushed back a loose strand of light-colored hair. She always wore her long hair tied up in a bun. She didn't part it down the middle like many women of the village did. Instead, she brushed it straight back from her forehead.

Mama set the full bowls on the table before saying, "Just think, your relatives from way back grew these berries, too.

Who knows…they might have brought seed with them when they came from Germany."

"That's a long time ago!" Anna exclaimed.

"The good thing about blackberries is that they're about as easy to grow as a weed," Mama laughed. She then got a sad look in her gray eyes before adding, "I'm going to miss our garden. I've spent a lot of hours caring for it."

In the afternoon, Anna watched as Mama washed the berries and drained the water off of them. Lots of seeds had settled to the bottom of her bowl. She carefully scooped them onto a clean cloth and sat them outdoors in the warm sunshine to dry. She then rolled out some bread dough for her strudel. She added some flour and sugar into the berries and spread the mixture over the dough. She pinched the edges shut, forming a long, wide roll before placing it into the oven. Soon the house smelled delicious.

The next two months passed quickly by for the Ertle family. "It's time to start packing," Mama announced. Like the rest of the villagers living in Volmer, Anna knew that their family didn't have a lot of clothes, but what they did have was very well made. In the cold, winter months, Papa didn't go out to his farm very often. Instead, he spent long hours working at his loom. He was a weaver of cloth. It fascinated her how separate threads could be intertwined to make beautiful material. Sometimes another man was seated next to him, learning the trade. Papa was known throughout the village as a weaving instructor, and she was proud of his skills.

Mama assisted Papa by spinning thread. She also made new garments for their family from what he wove. The rest of the cloth was sold, because money was needed to buy necessities for their household.

"I really like the scarf you made for me," Anna said as she folded it up.

21

"When we get to Ellis Island, we are going to dress in our very best clothes," Mama informed her.

"Why are we going to do that?"

"Because we want to make a good first impression," her mother explained.

The trunk was starting to get full. The only clothes that weren't folded up and packed away in it were the ones they were wearing. Anna was about to close the lid when Mama stopped her. "We're going to put the garden seeds in now," she said. She then proceeded to wrap her wool shawl around the pouches. As she carefully placed it into one corner of the trunk, she remarked, "Don't want the seeds to get wet. That would ruin them."

"Did you put the blackberry seeds in there, too?" Anna asked.

"No...I forgot!" Mama exclaimed, throwing her hands up into the air. "It's a good thing you said something! I stored them in a different cupboard than the rest of the seeds. That's why I didn't remember them." She carefully tucked the homemade pouch inside the black shawl with the others and closed the heavy lid.

The next morning, it was Sunday. Like usual, the family walked to church even though it was very cold. It felt good to get inside the warm building. As Anna walked down the aisle, she realized this would be the last time they would be worshipping there. Before Mass started, she looked around the church as if it were the first time she had ever seen it. It wasn't, of course, since she had been going there regularly since she was a newborn baby.

The congregation stood up to sing the first hymn. While they were singing, she glanced around at familiar faces. The Gartner family, who lived right across the street from them, was seated in the pew in front of them. She wondered why they were staying in Russia.

When the priest prayed for a safe journey for their family, it made Anna feel awkward. He also said a prayer for the Beilman family, who were going to be traveling on the same ship with them. He'd obviously been told that both families would be leaving on the long journey to America first thing in the morning.

After Mass was over, Joseph Gartner was the first to speak with the Ertle family. "Sure am going to miss you as neighbors," he said.

"Perhaps you should come to America, too," Mama replied. "My husband thinks it's time us German-Russians leave this country before it's too late."

"And he's right," Joseph agreed. "We're probably not going to be far behind you. The timing just isn't quite right for us. Maybe next year it will be."

"Well, I hope if you do decide to move you'll think about settling near Iliff, Colorado. My husband wrote in his letter that others from Volmer have put down roots there."

"I'll keep that in mind," Joseph commented. "Don't hesitate to ask if you need anything. We'd be glad to help however we can."

"Thank you, but we're already packed and ready to go," Mama said gratefully.

Before long, a crowd of well-wishers surrounded Anna's family. After plenty of hugs and sad goodbyes, they walked along the familiar streets of Volmer back to their home.

That night, Anna had a hard time trying to fall asleep. She tossed and turned. She was thinking about leaving Volmer, riding on a fast train, being on a big steamship, sailing over a huge, scary ocean and seeing Papa again. Without even realizing what happened, she drifted off to sleep.

Morning came early. "Anna, wake up. I need you to dress the younger kids while I get breakfast ready. Your grandpa and grandma will be here within the hour."

A sleepy Anna knew that would be true, because her grandparents were always on time. In fact, they usually arrived at places early.

About 45 minutes later, she heard a horse whinny outside their front door. She knew they had come to take them by wagon to Saratov. That is where they would board a train. Mama greeted her parents with a cheerful, "Good morning." She then reached for her handkerchief and began dabbing her eyes. "Wish you were going with us."

"We're too old," Grandpa replied matter-of-factly. "We wouldn't make it through the inspection process. We've heard how tough it is."

"We sure are going to miss you and the grandkids," Grandma commented, as she reached down to smooth Myrtle's hair.

"I know it'll be out of our way, but can you take us by our farm?" Mama asked. "I want to see it one more time."

"Then we best be leaving shortly," Grandpa replied. He got busy and started loading their things into the wagon.

Just as soon as everyone was aboard, Mama fussed, "I better go back into the house and check to make sure we didn't forget anything." When she came back outside, she lovingly shut the door behind her. Their home wouldn't be empty for long. Anna knew another family was planning on moving into it shortly. They would also be farming their land.

It was late October, and the morning air was crisp. Anna loved the peacefulness and beauty of the countryside. As the horses pulled the wagon by their farm, she remembered how hard Papa had worked in their fields. She wished Grandpa would pull back on the reins and command his horses to stop with a loud, "Whoa!" But she didn't dare speak her thoughts. Her parents had made a decision to move on, and they knew best.

The wagon ride took a long time, and the road was bumpy. Fortunately, they arrived at the train station with some time to spare. Anna listened quietly as Mama, Grandpa and Grandma talked about many things. It was grown-up conversation mostly, but she didn't mind. They probably had plenty to say and so little time to say it in.

5
S. S. Kursk

The Russian countryside was speeding past the train's windows. For the Ertle and Beilman families, Volmer was getting further and further away. Anna was glad that her mother had a young couple to travel with. They only had one son, who was two-years-old. Since Papa couldn't be there, it would have been almost impossible for Mama to make such a long journey without their help.

The clatter of the train's wheels was like a never-ending song. Ten-year-old Anna was tired of sitting, but she didn't dare complain. Mama was getting asked often enough by her younger sisters and brother, "How much longer till we get there?" She was old enough to know it would only mean switching from one form of travel to another.

The hours passed slowly, but finally the locomotive came to a jerky stop. "We're in port city of Libau," Mama informed her. "It's time to get off the train. This is where our steamship is going to depart."

Both families had a trunk and a large sack, which was stuffed with their personal belongings. Anna watched as

Mr. Beilman unloaded the heavy trunks. About that time, a young Russian man with a dark beard came up to him and asked, "Do you want me to haul them to the dock for you?"

Mr. Beilman quickly shook his head and replied, "Don't know what you're charging, but we can't afford it. Little hard work never hurt anyone. I'll manage."

With that, he tipped his hat as if to say thanks for the offer. He struggled to get the trunks moved to the loading dock, but he got the task accomplished.

Since the ship wasn't leaving for a while, they had time to eat. It was noon, and everyone was hungry. They found a small restaurant and went inside. Although it was packed with customers, the food didn't taste very good. "I can't believe how much it cost," Mama complained.

"They know traveling people have to eat somewhere," Mr. Beilman replied. "So they can charge more."

They then waited in line to get their basic physical examinations done. A doctor was screening the passengers. If someone failed, they wouldn't be allowed to board the ship.

After the two families passed their physicals, they were directed to wait in another line to receive the required shots. When it was Anna's turn, she cranked her head off to one side so she couldn't see the needle. The man told her, "Roll up your sleeve. I'm going to give you three different shots." He didn't tell her what the inoculations were meant to prevent. Her stomach got a little queasy feeling with the first prick of a needle. She was glad when the man was through with her. She then turned around to console her crying sister Lena, who was getting poked with a needle.

Before long, they were waiting in another line, and it was moving slowly. The early afternoon sun felt warm on Anna's shoulders. She glanced over at the huge ship that was docked at the edge of the ocean. It had two tall smokestacks towering above it. When Mama bought their tickets to travel on the S. S. Kursk, the company told her that the ship was built in 1911. It had just started carrying passengers across the ocean from Russia to the Golden Land that year. The outside of the ship still looked brand new. She hoped it would be nice inside, too.

At last, they made their way up to a pretty lady, who was seated at a small table. She was asking the Beilmans lots of questions and writing their answers down in a big, important-looking book. Anna noticed that her writing was beautiful. The letters were fancily formed. The young German-Russian girl wished she could write that way. Maybe they would teach her how when she got to school in America.

When the lady asked her mother a question, Mama had one of her own, "Why do you need to know all of this?"

"I have to put it on the ship manifest," the lady replied. "It lists all the passengers on board, where they've come from and where they're going." She then asked, "What's your age?"

"Thirty," Mama replied reluctantly. "I don't see why you need that information."

"It's my job, but I do understand how you feel. I also have to ask what your profession is."

"Housewife," Mama answered with obvious frustration. "What else could I be?"

"A mother with six very good-looking children," she answered. "I also must list their names and ages." After getting everything she needed, the lady smiled and handed Mama seven cards. "These are your manifest tags. They are numbered 13 through 19, and they match the lines where you are listed on the manifest. The tags will help avoid identification problems later on in the journey."

The Ertles and Beilmans then walked up an angled plank. An older man was standing on the deck. He asked to see their passports and tickets. After looking over the paperwork, he said smugly, "Steerage passengers…you'll be traveling on the lower deck at the back part of the ship. Follow the signs that are written in both German and Russian."

When the two families arrived in their sleeping quarters, Anna looked around at the other people in the area. It was crowded down there. Everyone looked poor, just like their two families did. "Where did the rich people go?" Anna asked.

"They're cabin class passengers," Mr. Beilman replied. "They get to stay in the nicer part of the ship, but they had to pay a lot more money than we did to travel. We're just poor folks. It's not going to be a pleasant trip down here, but we'll survive."

Anna watched as more and more families continued to flock in. The room looked like it was shrinking. The walls were closing in around her. To escape the confusion, she climbed up on the top bunk. The bed had an iron frame. Mama had previously told her that is where she would be sleeping during the voyage. She was just sitting there when she began feeling movement. The steamer was headed out to the vast Atlantic Ocean. They were leaving the huge country of Russia, and the life they were familiar with behind. She didn't know whether to be sad or happy.

It didn't take long for the motion to get to Anna's stomach. She was feeling queasy. Before she knew what happened, she lost her lunch. She was ashamed that she never made it to the bathroom in time, and she began crying. Mama came over and wiped away her salty tears. "I'm afraid this is going to be a long journey for you," she said soothingly. She then began cleaning up the wood floor.

Unfortunately, Anna wasn't alone. Her brother and sisters all got seasick except for Myrtle. It was a good thing Mama wasn't ill, because she was kept busy caring for her children. The endless motion was making a lot of the steerage passengers seasick. The area smelled awful. "Why don't you kids try to get some sleep," Mama encouraged them. "Maybe you'll feel better when you wake up."

So Anna crawled under her thin blanket and covered up her nose. She wasn't really tired, but she finally managed to drift off. As she slept, dreams that didn't make any sense kept coming one after another.

When she woke up, she felt cold and confused. It took her a moment to realize she was on the S. S. Kursk, which was sailing toward America. A few adults were standing in the corner talking, but most were resting or busy doing things in their bunk beds. Mama was sitting in hers, reading her prayer book. The big sack that was filled with their possessions was beside her. "Are you going to keep our belongings in your bed during the whole trip?" Anna asked.

"I'll have to. There's no place to store them on this ship."

"But you won't have much room to sleep in," Anna pointed out.

"I'll manage," Mama assured her. "Been through tougher times than this. Besides, it's nice to have our things handy. Never know what I'll need. Just hope our trunk remains safe. Mr. Beilman is going to check on the trunks every once in a while."

The next morning, Anna, her brother and sisters were feeling better. "They're serving breakfast. Let's get in line," Mama told them. "You need to get some food into your bellies and keep up your strength. The last thing I need is for you kids to get really sick."

"But we've already been sick," Anna corrected her.

"Lots of people get seasick. That's pretty normal," Mama explained. "If one of us has something contagious when we get to Ellis Island, they might deport us."

"You mean they'd send our whole family back to Russia?" Anna asked. Her blue eyes widened with fear. She hadn't thought of that as a possibility.

"They can do whatever they want," Mama replied honestly, "and we can't do much about it."

Three stewards were putting breakfast foods on the passengers' plates so the line moved fairly quickly. For the first time since Anna stepped on board, she was hungry. Since there weren't enough wooden tables for everyone to sit down and eat their meals, the men stood up next to the wall while they ate.

After Mr. Beilman was finished with his breakfast, he came over and said, "Sure would feel good to get some fresh air. I'm tired of feeling like a cooped up animal. If we hurry, there might be some standing room up on the deck."

The two families joined a crowd of people who all had the same idea. Anna was amazed at how huge the waves were. For as far as she could see, there was an endless sea of water. She didn't know how to swim so the ocean really frightened her.

"Oh, so much water," Mama observed. "I'm already tired of seeing only water. We're farmers; we feel at home on the land."

Anna agreed. She was ready to put her feet down on dry ground. She also missed having a home. It seemed like Papa had left for America a long time ago. It was hard for her to remember exactly what his voice sounded like. She was anxious to be a complete family once again.

6
Ellis Island

Monday morning, November 20, 1911, the Ertle family got up at the crack of dawn to dress in their best clothes. "I feel like I should be going to church," Anna remarked.

"It's going to be a big day for us," Mama replied breathlessly. She was hurriedly dressing two-year-old Mary. "The Beilmans are waiting on us. We're going up on deck so we can see our first glimpse of the Golden Land."

Shortly after that, the two families joined a sea of passengers. The fresh air felt wonderful, but there were too many people for Anna's liking. She felt like a sardine.

Before long, a man caught her attention when he shouted, "There's the Statue of Liberty!" She looked in the direction he was pointing and saw a tall monument. As they got closer, she thought it looked like the huge lady was wearing a green dress. Her right arm was raised way above her head. Anna imagined that the lady was waving to all those who had left Russia to come to America. She was welcoming the strangers to the shore she proudly stood over.

A woman passenger got her attention when she shouted, "That must be Ellis Island! See that huge, red brick building with the gray trim; I think that's the building we'll have to go through to get accepted into this country."

There was plenty of excitement when the steamship docked. The journey over the Atlantic Ocean had taken them 13 long days. Everyone was anxious to get off of the ship, but another steamer had arrived shortly before them. They would have to wait their turn. Meanwhile, customs inspectors boarded the S. S. Kursk. Steerage passengers were given coded inspection cards, which were pinned to their clothing. The numbers on them corresponded to the ship's manifest page and line where their name and information was listed.

The customs inspectors divided the steerage passengers into groups of 30. They were told that is the number of people and belongings a barge could hold. They were strictly instructed to stay together as a unit during the entire immigration process. Anna listened as Mrs. Beilman told Mama, "I'm so glad we got in the same group as you did. At least, we'll know someone."

After what seemed like a very long wait, it was their turn to be ferried over to the main building. They were dropped off at the front entrance. "You must stay near me at all times!" Mama firmly instructed her children. "Anna, grab hold of Lena's hand, and don't let loose of it! She's only four-years-old. We don't want her wandering off."

Mr. Beilman's strength was called upon as he carried their heavy trunks into the baggage room to be checked in. "I worry about leaving our trunks unattended," Mama fretted. "What if someone takes them?"

"Don't know who you can trust," Mr. Beilman replied, "but we don't have a choice. We'll carry our big bags with us, but the trunks have to stay here."

Anna definitely felt like she was in a whole new world. She was absorbing the action around her. She listened to people talking in languages she couldn't understand. She studied the way they were dressed. Up until now, she thought all people were nearly the same. Course, she had rarely ventured out of the German-Russian village where she had grown up.

Her thoughts were interrupted when an Ellis Island guide directed them, "Take this central stairway up to the registry room. There you'll be given a medical exam, which includes both physical and mental evaluations, and a legal exam. Good luck to you."

At the top of the stairs, an attendant stamped their inspection cards. Anna noticed that the registry room had been divided up into many small subdivisions by using fencing. It was made out of pipes and wire. In each section, there was a cluster of people. She had never seen anything like that before. It reminded her of animals being penned up. Their group soon found themselves in one of the partitioned off sections. They were instructed to move forward when the people ahead of them did. Eventually, they would work their way up to where the doctor was examining the aliens.

Mama gladly sat down on a bench and cradled a sleepy Mary in her arms. "This is by far the biggest room I've ever been in, and it's packed with people. We're going to be here forever."

Anna had to agree. The room was gigantic, and its ceilings were very high. Still, it felt crowded, because of all the people crammed in there. As they waited, the young German-Russian girl watched the doctor at work. She could tell he was checking every immigrant's eyes and hair. Occasionally, he picked up a piece of chalk and wrote a letter on the passenger's clothing. That person was then escorted into another room. "Is it bad if you get a chalk mark?" she asked.

Mama shrugged her shoulders, but Mrs. Beilman quickly answered. "I've heard it was. The letter stands for what health issue you have. If it's bad enough, they'll deport you back to Russia on the same ship you came over on." Anna knew that was the biggest fear Mama had – she didn't want to be deported.

When at last it was time for Anna to be examined by the doctor, she barely breathed. She definitely didn't want him to pick up his piece of chalk. She was glad when the exam was over. She could see the relief in Mama's tired face when everyone in their family had made it through the medical exam without any trouble. The Beilmans had passed, as well.

Their group then had to weave its way through the cattle-like pens over to the west side of the room. Once again, it was a slow process. When the Beilman family reached the front of the line, an interpreter fired question after question at Mr. Beilman in German. He then conveyed his answers to the inspector.

In a few minutes, they were admitted into the United States. They received landing cards and were free to go wherever they pleased. The couple shared their joy by giving each other a big hug.

The Beilmans waited while questions were directed toward Mama. Anna listened as the interpreter asked her mother's full name, age, whether she was married or single, plus more questions. When he asked her if she could read or write in English, she replied, "No, but I can read and write in Low German."

The last question the interpreter asked Mama was if a responsible male was there to pick up the family. "No," she admitted honestly. "My husband is at home in Iliff, Colorado." She pointed over to the Beilmans and continued,

"Since this family is going there, too, he told me to travel with them. I have money for our railroad tickets."

It soon became obvious the answers Mama gave didn't satisfy the inspector. The interpreter told her the bad news, "Sorry, Ma'am. Your family is going to be detained."

"What does that mean?"

"You're going to be held at Ellis Island until you go before the Board of Special Inquiry. That should be in about two weeks. They'll ask you more questions to determine whether you'll be admitted into the United States or deported back to Russia. In the meantime, I'll help you fill out this postcard. It costs you nothing to have us mail it to your husband. Ellis Island offers it as a service to those who have been detained. What is his address?"

All journey long, Mama had been carrying a small bag, which contained important papers. She pulled out the letter Papa had written her and handed it to the interpreter. He wrote the address on the postcard before saying, "The printed message on the card will let your husband know you've arrived safely at Ellis Island, but you're being detained. It will advise him to pick up his family if he chooses to. I will add a note telling him that he should bring the postcard with him. It will make it a lot easier for us to put him in contact with his family."

"Thank you," Mama said humbly. She then added adamantly, "He'll come!"

"I'm sure he will," the interpreter replied. "The board wants to make sure that a male will care for your family. They don't want you to become a public charge to the government. Your husband won't be allowed to talk with you before the hearing, but he can give testimony to the Board of Special Inquiry after they question you if he needs to."

For a moment, Mama was speechless. Finally, she asked, "Where do we go in the meantime?"

"We have dormitory rooms where those who are being held spend the night," the interpreter explained. "In the morning, your family will be brought back to the detention room. Meals will be served at no cost. Detainees are expected to occupy themselves the best they can. There are some restrictions on where you can go. You are allowed up on the rooftop for exercise. There is a playground up there for the children. You can also go into the religious room. All denominations can use it."

"I feel so bad for you," Mrs. Beilman said sincerely. "I'm sure the board will admit you once they know your husband is here."

"I hope so," Mama said with tears welling up in her eyes.

"Everything is going to work out fine," Mr. Beilman reassured her. "You've just run into a bump in the road."

After saying their goodbyes, Mr. and Mrs. Beilman and their two-year-old son went their own way, and the Ertle family was ushered off to the dining room. It was suppertime, and Anna was starved. As the food was being dished up on their plates, she couldn't help but blurt out, "What's this? We've never eaten anything like it before!"

The lady who was doing the serving replied, "Spaghetti…Americans eat that kind of food."

It looked like worms to Anna. She really didn't like it, but she cleaned her plate. She'd been taught not to waste food.

After the family finished their meal, they were escorted back to their dormitory room. It was a nice, clean room. Everyone was ready for bed. It had been a very long day without the ending they'd hoped for.

In the next several days, the family got into a routine. Right after breakfast, Anna watched her brother and sisters in the detention room while Mama spent some quiet time in the religious room. She went there to pray and gain inner strength for the coming day. After they ate their noon meal, the family went to the rooftop where Mama walked and the children enjoyed the playground equipment. The fresh air felt wonderful and so did the warmth of the midday sun. From their vantage point, they could see for miles, but they weren't free to leave the building on which they stood.

"It doesn't seem fair that we have to stay here," Anna grumbled.

"I know what you mean," Mama agreed. "The people we see down below are busy living their lives. That's all I want."

The day the hearing was scheduled for finally arrived. Anna could tell that Mama was very nervous. When she wasn't busy meeting the needs of one of her kids, she sat there quietly and wrung her hands. Even though she was in a room filled with other people, she looked so alone. When a man came into the room and announced, "Mrs. Ertle, please gather your children, and follow me to the board room," she quickly stood up.

Mama had a serious, determined look on her face as they entered the official- looking room. Three men were solemnly seated on one side of a long table. The Ertles were motioned to find seats on the other side of it. Once again, an interpreter directed questions to Mama in German. This time she answered them with a lot more confidence than before. When they asked her about employment, she replied, "My husband says we'll be working for a farmer in his sugar beet fields. We'll do what we have to in order to make a living. We don't want a handout, nor would we ever take one."

One of the men then said, "Let's take our vote." All three of them said yes. The same man smiled before explaining their verdict, "You're a strong, determined woman. America is the land of opportunity. We believe you and your family will make the best of that privilege. You've been admitted into the United States of America for permanent residence. Here are your landing cards. We were told that your husband is anxiously waiting for you in the next room. I'm sure you'd love to see him."

"We most certainly would!" Mama exclaimed merrily. "It's been a long time since we've seen him. Thank you." Anna thought her mother looked like the world's burdens had just been lifted off of her shoulders. The family was soon joyfully reunited with Papa, making everything seem right once again.

America was giving them a chance to start over, and it was up to them to make the most of it. With their landing cards proudly displayed on their clothing, the family of eight proceeded down to the railway ticket office. They needed to purchase tickets for their trip to Iliff, Colorado.

The last piece of business the Ertles had at Ellis Island was to reclaim their trunk in the baggage area. Mama was pleased that it was still there and was unharmed. They weren't going to begin a new life in America with much, but the immigrant family would make sure it was enough.

7
Johannes
Suz's grandfather on her father's side

It was July of 1912. The Gartner family would be leaving Volmer in about a month. They were going to join the wave of immigrants, who were seeking a better life in America.

Fifteen-year-old Johannes was their second oldest son. He stood at the edge of their wheat field, gazing out across it. Heavy heads of grain swayed in the breeze. He knew his father was counting on a bountiful harvest. In the past few days, the hot sun had turned the stalks into a beautiful golden color. For as long as he could remember, he'd dreamed of becoming a farmer. The magnificent scene before him made him want to farm even more. Since this was going to be their last year of growing crops on Russian soil, he felt like his dream might never happen. He had no idea what was in store for him in America.

While the dark-haired young man wished he could stay and soak up the peacefulness of the countryside a while longer, he knew it was getting close to suppertime. His blue eyes captured one last image of the beauty God had created before heading back to the village.

The next morning at the crack of dawn, the Gartners left their village and headed out to their farm. Wheat harvest was a family affair for them. They would be gathering the wheat into sheaves by hand, which was time-consuming work. Dad, Mom and all seven kids, including the three-year-old twins, were prepared to stay out in the field until the work was completed. The farm was located a good distance from the village so they took along a supply of food and plenty to drink.

By the time they arrived at their twenty-acre wheat field, their two neighbors were already there. Dad had hired them to cut the grain. Within minutes, the workhorses began pulling the raff (mowing machine) that was efficiently slicing down the golden stems. It took two men to operate the labor-saving machine.

Johannes enjoyed working alongside his father. He admired how fast Dad knotted two handfuls of stalks together at the stubble end, forming a long band. With his free arm, he scooped up a large armful of wheat and wrapped his handmade band firmly around the middle of the bundle. He then quickly twisted the kernel ends together and tucked them under. His sheaf was tightly tied and neatly made. Without pausing, he would immediately start on a new one. "How do you do that so fast?" an inquisitive Johannes wanted to know.

His father laughed before replying, "Lots and lots of practice. I remember when we used scythes to cut the wheat stalks."

"That had to be hard, dangerous work," Johannes reasoned.

"Yep, I'm glad those days are behind us," Dad replied.

Johannes glanced over at his mom and older brother Joe,

who were working nearby. They were also busy gathering stalks of grain and tying them into sheaves. Dad expected the younger kids George, Lizzie and Pauline to follow behind and do the shocking. He showed them how to set ten sheaves upright on their butt ends, forming a tight group. He demonstrated how to make a roof by spreading out the stems of two sheaves and draping them over the other bundles like an umbrella. They did this in case it rained. When the shock was made correctly, it would allow the grain and straw to dry completely and keep the wind from blowing the sheaves over. All of the wheat had to be shocked before they went home. They couldn't leave it lying on the ground overnight, because the dew would cause the kernels to spoil.

Even though they were busy working, there was plenty of talking, kidding and laughing going on amongst the family members. Anna and Alex, the twins, were too young to help. They played with rocks, sticks, whatever they could find out in the field. Occasionally, Mom took a short break to give them some attention.

Johannes stopped working for a moment to wipe the sweat off of his forehead. "Is the wheat as good as you hoped?" he asked.

"We've been blessed with an above average crop," Dad replied. "Since we're moving, a couple of the older farmers have already asked me if I'd sell them some seed wheat. I told them that I would."

"Aren't we going to take some with us?" Johannes questioned his father's thinking.

"No need to," Dad replied quickly. "We won't be farming on our own in Colorado. Not at first anyway. When Jacob (a close relative) wrote a while back, he said that he had work waiting for us. We'll be working for a farmer as laborers out in his sugar beet fields. He says they raise some dry land wheat, but beets are their main crop. So there wouldn't be any point in hauling seed to America that we won't need. It would just take up lots of room in our trunk, and we've got limited space."

"I know Mom is planning on taking garden seeds with us," Johannes mentioned.

"Yes," Dad chuckled. "She's even joked with me that she won't leave Russia if she can't take them with us. She loves her garden."

"Isn't Mom looking forward to going to America?"

"I think she's worried about the big change. She likes her routine," Dad expressed his opinion. "I don't care for change, either, but things aren't good here. The Russian government is getting to be something else. It'll probably take her a while to adjust once we're in America, but we've got relatives living over there already. That will help. Plus, we know lots of other families that used to live in Volmer, like the Ertles. We'll find a small patch of ground somewhere to grow us a nice garden. Then she'll feel right at home."

The rest of the morning passed quickly by. The hot sun had maneuvered its way directly overhead, and Johannes could tell by the growl in his stomach that it was dinnertime. He was hungry! Dad invited the two neighbor men to join them. Mom had cooked a big batch of homemade wurst (German sausage) the night before. They ate the cold meat in between slices of rye bread. It tasted delicious. "Working hard certainly gives everyone a much better appetite," Mom observed.

Mealtime didn't last long. Dad got back up on his feet, stretched his weary back and legs and said, "The quicker we get started; the sooner we'll get finished."

A few hours later, the mowing had been completed. Dad took off his straw hat and waved at the two neighbors. It was as if he was saying goodbye to them and thanks all at the same time. Johannes didn't know for sure, but he figured they would be cutting another farmer's field early the next morning.

As the powerful workhorses pulled the mowing machine out of the field, the young man watched. He could tell that the horses were well-trained as they lumbered on down the road. He admired their brown coats, which looked slick and shiny. Dad got his attention when he yelled over to him, "Good workhorses are like a smooth-running machine. They'll work hard for you as long as you take good care of them."

"Aren't you going to be sad when we have to sell our workhorses before we leave for America?"

"It'll be like leaving a part of our family behind," Dad expressed his innermost feelings. Then he took a long, deep sigh.

Johannes was surprised. He rarely saw his father get emotional, and it made him feel a bit uncomfortable.

"I'll make sure I sell them to someone who'll take good care of them," Dad added with renewed optimism. As the day wore on, Johannes was impressed by how many shocks dotted the field. They looked like stacks of money to him. He was aware of the fact that their family needed quite a bit of money to make the long trip to America. There were railroad and steamship tickets to buy. Plus, his dad had to pay their neighbors for mowing their field.

In the late afternoon, Dad gathered the family around him before saying, "We've still got plenty of wheat lying on the ground; we need to push a little harder so we can finish up before it gets dark. There isn't going to be much of a moon out tonight."

Johannes heard his younger sister Pauline moan before saying, "I'm tired. I just want to go home."

"We'll work a little while longer, and then we'll eat a quick supper," Mom told her. "You can rest then."

Johannes was tired, too. He understood his sister's complaint. Being out in the wind and the sun all day long had taken its toil on the whole family. He knew his father wouldn't go home before the job was finished. There was no way his parents were going to let good wheat spoil on the ground. When they got back to work, he did his best to pick up the slack for his sister.

Supper was a repeat of dinner. They sat on the ground eating German sausage sandwiches. Dad always ate extremely fast whenever work was waiting for him. Tonight was no exception. He was already finished eating when he spoke, "We haven't got a whole lot left. We should be done within an hour. Our beds at home are going to feel mighty good tonight." Just as soon as he got up, Johannes followed his lead. He didn't mind that the rest of the family took a little longer rest period.

Right before sunset, they finished up with the shocking. Everyone was exhausted for it had been a very long day. Darkness would soon be creeping in. It was time to head back to the village and get a good night's rest. That part of wheat harvest was behind them. The dusty part of threshing lay ahead.

A few days later, Dad hitched up a team of workhorses to their druska (cart). He hauled the sheaves to their barn. Johannes, his brothers Joe and George helped their father knock the kernels free with flails. The wheat was then sacked. Normally, they would save a small portion of their crop to take to the mill to be ground into flour. Not this harvest, though. There was no need to do so. Mom had enough rye flour to last until they left for America. Dad separated out the seed wheat like he'd promised the two farmers and sold the rest of it to the village grain elevator.

One evening at supper, Mom announced happily, "Lizzie and Pauline picked enough ripe schwartzbeeren (blackberries) for me to make a couple of pies. I also saved seeds to take on our trip to America."

"The time will be here before you know it," Dad said. And it was.

On an August morning, Mom's parents came to the house to take them to Saratov. Grandpa and Grandma had no plans of ever leaving Volmer. They were staying put, where they expected to live out the rest of their lives.

As Grandpa's horses pulled the wagon down the road, Johannes got nostalgic. "We're giving up free land that Russia handed my ancestors years ago. If only things were different, I would have farmed here, too," he thought. He sat there quietly and watched the countryside go by mile after mile.

After the long trip, it was time to say farewell. "I don't like goodbyes, especially this one," Grandma expressed with tears streaming down her face.

When Grandpa spoke, tears filled his eyes, "We'll see you in Heaven." Johannes got a lump in his throat. This really was their final goodbye to one another. They wouldn't see each other face-to-face in this country or on earth ever again. The distance between them would soon become too great to travel.

The nine of them boarded the train with heavy hearts and were soon on their way to Liverpool, England. The next step of their journey would be on the S. S. Laconia. They would be traveling as lowly steerage passengers. Unlike many of the other German-Russian families who had left before them, the Gartners weren't going to sail to Ellis Island. They would be landing at a Boston port. They'd heard this inspection center didn't process nearly as many immigrants on a daily basis. Treatment of aliens was supposed to be much better there, plus it was a dollar cheaper to enter the country.

On September 11, 1912, their ship arrived at the eastern shoreline of America. The Gartners' fate would soon be decided by immigration authorities.

Alex, one of the twins, was only three-years-old on the historic occasion. Of course, he couldn't remember going through the immigration center, but his parents told him about it when he got older. Many years later, he wrote an article about the family's experience in a centennial history book, "After getting a clean bill of health from immigration authorities, we boarded a train and traveled by rail across the great country of America until we arrived at our destination of Iliff, Colorado. Here we were met by our sponsor Jacob Gartner (a close relative) who had work and a place for us to stay. Thus, we joined other Germans from Russia in the fields as laborers working beets."

8
Pete
Suz's grandfather on her mother's side

John Peter Lambrecht was born in Pfeifer, Russia on November 8, 1895. His great, great, great, great grandfather Sebastian had been an early settler of the village. The Catholic colony was established by hardy Germans in 1767. Through the years, Pfeifer grew to become one of the nicer, larger German-Russian villages in the Volga River Region.

By the summer of 1912, John Peter was better known around the village as Pete. The young man with light brown hair and blue eyes didn't give the past much thought. Instead, his focus was on the future. Come fall, Dad, Mom, his two sisters, three brothers and himself had plans to leave Pfeifer. They would be going on a long, difficult journey in search of a better life in America; but in the meantime, it was business as usual for them.

Early Saturday morning, Dad and Pete hitched the horses up to their wagon and traveled out to the farm to spend the day working out in the field. Late that afternoon,

Dad said, "Let's go check on Elsie. I noticed earlier that she'd gone to the far end of the pasture, and she's all by herself. I figure she's about ready to have her calf."

"That will make Mom happy," Pete remarked as they began walking at a steady pace through the pasture. "She's been complaining that she only has enough milk for us to drink. She doesn't have any extra to make butter or cottage cheese. Hilga's only been giving a half bucket of milk lately."

"It's time we let her go dry," Dad replied. "Just milk her in the evenings but not in the mornings for about a week or so. Then quit altogether. She'll be having another calf in a couple of months."

As they got closer to Elsie, they could already tell that she'd given birth. A black, wobbly-legged calf was trying its best to stand up. "It looks like a healthy heifer," Dad stated happily. "If we weren't moving to America, that's just what we would have wanted to build up our herd. Someone will gladly buy her."

The second Dad picked up the calf, the new mother began to moo loudly. She didn't want anyone handling her baby. On the way to their barn, Pete did his best to keep the protective cow away from his father. He hurriedly opened the barn door, and Dad put the newborn calf into a pen.

"I'll milk Elsie," Dad said. "You can milk Hilga."

Pete was relieved that his father wanted to milk the unhappy new mother. The large cow continued to moo, and she had no intentions of standing still. His father would have to be on his guard so that he didn't get kicked.

Meanwhile, Pete went back out to the pasture and herded Hilga into the barn. He fed her some ground up corn before sitting down on his homemade wooden stool beside her. He never grew tired of hearing the first squirts of milk, hitting an empty pail. He loved the smell of warm milk mingling with the odors of the barn. In a short time, he'd emptied the cow's bag. A layer of foam had formed over the top of the white liquid.

Pete watched as Dad finished milking. When he opened the barn door, he didn't have to slap Hilga on her flank; she was ready to go back outside. Elsie, on the other hand, was being stubborn. She desperately wanted to stay near her calf. It took both of them to force her out the door.

"I'll feed the calf," Pete volunteered.

"Okay," Dad replied, "and I'll go feed the pigs."

Pete picked up the bucket that contained the new mother's milk. It was a rich yellow color. It contained plenty of good nutrients to help the calf get its start in life. At this point, the family couldn't drink the milk; but in a few days, it would turn snow white. Then they would be able to use whatever the calf didn't need. He poured the milk into a nipple bucket and tried to get the calf to suck on it. The newborn didn't have a clue what it was supposed to do. So Pete dipped his fingers into the warm, sticky liquid and forced them into its mouth. It took patience, but he finally got a fair amount of nutrition down the calf. He knew in a few days that the heifer would be drinking eagerly.

Dad stepped back into the barn. "When you're finished, let's call it a day, Son. It's getting late. Hopefully, we get home before your mother has supper on the table."

"I'm ready to go," he replied before picking up the pail of milk that Hilga had given.

When they got home, Pete handed Mom the pail. He watched as she put a clean cloth over a pitcher and began pouring the white liquid into it. He'd made every effort not to get dirt into the milk, but his mother always strained it as an added precaution. "Elsie had her calf today," he stated.

"Good," she answered. "I can use it." She sat the pitcher on the table and finished preparing supper.

Before they ate their meal, Pete silently prayed his before meal prayer in German. It never even seemed strange to him that he had lived his entire life in Russia, yet he didn't know a single Russian prayer. German was the only language that Dad and Mom spoke in their household. Most of the customs they followed in their home were those of their ancestors. It was as if they were living in a land without a country to claim as their own.

Mom broke the silence around the table when she expressed her concern, "We don't have a lot of canned meats left."

"Do you have enough to get by with until we leave for America?" Dad asked.

"I'll have to stretch it," she replied.

"We'll just have to make do," Dad emphasized. "No point in butchering anything now." He hesitated a moment before adding, "Joe Kippes says he'll buy all of our pigs. Most of them are getting close to butchering weight."

"These past few days, the weather has gotten cold enough to butcher," Mom remarked. "If we were staying, I'd already be dreading all the work that goes with butchering."

Pete started thinking about the delicious head cheese his mother made, and his mouth began to water. She'd simmer the pig's head; and when the stock got cold, it would form a gel around the chunks of meat trimmings. "A slice of your head cheese sure would taste good right about now," he spoke up.

Rose, his oldest sister, quickly gave her opinion, "How can you stand to eat that stuff?"

"It's good!" Pete exclaimed. "You don't know what you're missing."

"I'm glad you like it," his mother replied. Her face was beaming at the compliment she had received about her cooking.

Early Sunday morning, Dad and Pete got up before the rest of the family. They had to go do the farm chores. On their way out of the house, his father grabbed the lantern. The sun hadn't risen above the eastern horizon, yet; but they almost didn't need the artificial light. When Pete glanced up, he saw a dark sky filled with an abundant sprinkling of brilliant stars and a half moon. As the horses pulled the wagon along the dirt road, only the sound of their hooves pounding on the ground could be heard. The air was crisp, and the surroundings were peaceful. It was one of those times when talking wasn't necessary to enjoy each other's company.

When they finished up with the chores, it was time to head back to the village. They ate a quick breakfast and changed into their nicest clothes before leaving for church.

The Church of St. Francis of Assisi was located in the center of their village. There was nothing fancy about the outside of the large building. It was constructed of wood, but the inside of the church was beautiful. It had a high altar and side altars that were decorated with elaborate wood carvings. They were finished in white, a pale blue and gold. There also were statues highlighted in gold. The upper inside walls had been whitewashed, while the lower halves of the walls were light blue. To Pete, the inside of their church looked like a piece of Heaven on earth.

On this Sunday morning the priest greeted the congregation before saying, "With so many of our members leaving and going to America, I think the following verse taken from Matthew 19:29 is very appropriate: And everyone who has left houses or brothers or sisters or father or mother or children or lands, for my name's sake, will receive a hundredfold and inherit eternal life."

Pete was thankful that the Russians hadn't taken away their freedom to worship. Since they'd gone back on other promises that Catherine the Great had originally granted them, many people felt it was absolutely necessary to leave the country. Perhaps it was only going to be a matter of time before they took their religious freedom away, too. He had heard some of the villagers voice their concerns about it.

During the next month, the Lambrechts began selling their livestock to new owners. Their workhorses, cows and pigs were taken away one by one or sometimes in groups. Pete hated to see them go. When they were all gone, an eerie quietness fell over their property.

When the family packed up their belongings, the reality of moving to another continent finally set in. The tiniest things they were bringing with them were schwartzbeeren (blackberry) seeds. They were the main ingredient in some of their ethnic foods so they didn't dare leave them behind.

At Saratov, they exchanged sad farewells with both sets of parents. As they boarded the train that was destined for Poland, Pete more clearly understood the Bible reading from Matthew. They really were leaving their house, fathers, mothers, land and much more behind. Up until now, they had invested their entire lives into making a home in Russia. It hadn't worked out, and it was time to move forward before it was too late.

Once the Lambrechts arrived in Poland, the family of eight went by ship to England. In Liverpool, they boarded the S. S. Dominion on October 30th, which was bound for America. It wasn't pleasant to be a steerage passenger, and Pete voiced his opinion, "I think we took better care of our animals than we're being treated. They need to clean the ship more often."

"It's only temporary," Dad replied. "We'll just have to make the best out of it."

After seemingly endless days of traveling, the steamship docked at Philadelphia on November 11, 1912. They'd reached their destination exhausted and confused, but they had arrived! With apprehension, they went through the immigration center. They'd been dreading the medical and legal exams. It was a relief when they were officially admitted into America.

They purchased railroad tickets with a destination of Topeka, Kansas. There, they made their home until May of the following year. The Lambrechts then moved to northeastern Colorado where the family was truly able to establish new, permanent roots.

9
Magdalena
Suz's grandmother on her mother's side

The village of Schuck, Russia was located to the northwest of Pfeifer where Pete grew up. When his family immigrated to America, he had no idea that a girl from Schuck, who had dark brown hair and hazel eyes, would someday be his bride.

For Magdalena Hochnadel, the German Catholic village became her home twice in her lifetime. In 1904, she was five-years-old. She was old enough to remember the first time they left Schuck. She along with Dad, Mom and her three sisters boarded a steamship destined for San Jose, Argentina.

For as long as she lived, Magdalena would never forget the terrible day when Mom gave birth to a new baby boy aboard the ship. For reasons unknown to her, Phillip's life ended almost before it began. Her mother was heartbroken. It was up to Dad to take the bundled, lifeless body up on deck and toss his firstborn son out into the cold, murky water. It didn't seem right to bury him at sea, but her father had no choice. As the man of the family, he did what needed to be done. If only, he was as good at consoling his loved one in her grief. Magdalena didn't like seeing Mom so sad. The rest of the voyage to South America was a long, dreary one.

After being in Argentina for seven years, Dad found it extremely difficult to make a living. The scouting reports he'd heard before they moved to South America had sounded much more promising. Money was very short, and he was growing restless. Magdalena didn't know what to think when she heard her dejected father say, "I think it's time we give up and move on."

"You don't have to convince me," Mom replied. "I don't want to spend the rest of my life here, either, but where will we go?"

"Some of our people went to the United States, others have gone to Canada," he answered, "I don't have any idea how we would go about traveling to those countries from here. If we go back to Russia, all we have to do is communicate with your parents by letters. They'll gladly pick us up at the train station." The subject was then dropped abruptly.

Magdalena had forgotten about the possibility of moving until one morning at breakfast when Dad announced, "We're going back to Schuck. At least we know the territory and the people. We still have family living there."

Mom chimed in, "Russia certainly wasn't a perfect place to live, but it was better than this. It feels so alone here. I miss family."

"Do you think they'll remember us?" Magdalena asked.

"Oh yes!" Mom exclaimed. "You don't forget those you love."

In 1911, the Hochnadels packed up their worldly possessions and boarded a steamship bound for Russia. It was like they were reversing the path they'd taken seven years prior. The next step on their journey was by train. It raced across the countryside. At last the wheels came to a halt, and they descended down the train's steps.

Like planned, Mom's parents were there to meet them. After Grandma wiped away a few tears, she remarked, "It's so good to see you all again. Let me take a good long look at our three new grandchildren."

"This is Barbara. She's five already," Mom said, pointing over at her shy daughter. "And this is Anna Marie. She's two. Of course, the baby is Andrew."

Before long, Grandma took Andrew out of Mom's arms and held him. "They're all beautiful children!" she exclaimed.

Grandpa put his finger on the baby's open palm. The pudgy, little hand squeezed it. "We can't make up for lost time, but we can enjoy what we have right here and now."

When Grandma saw Magdalena standing in the background, she exclaimed, "I can't believe how you've grown! You look like your mother when she was a girl."

A blushing Magdalena looked over at Mom and giggled before replying, "I don't think I look like her."

"Yes, you do," Grandpa agreed. It was obvious that he was anxious to get on the road when he added, "We've got a long wagon ride ahead of us. We best get started. We can talk all the way back to Schuck."

"Lots of people in the village have been asking us when you're coming back," Grandma informed them. "They're all excited to see you."

"Mom said they'd be happy to see us," Magdalena said.

"Your family has been missed more than you'll ever know," Grandma replied.

When they got to Schuck, Magdalena enjoyed all the attention their family received. Before she knew what happened, they were settled into their daily lives. Dad and

Mom were kept busy with the work that went into running a farm and household. The first year that they were back in Russia flew quickly by and began blending into the following one.

On a spring afternoon in 1913, Mom was getting ready to make some grebble (German dessert similar to fried doughtnuts.) Magdalena enjoyed watching her cook so she started to pull out a chair to sit down at the table. "You can help," her mother insisted. "You're almost fourteen-years-old. How else are you going to learn?"

The teenager had never made grebble before. It was one of her favorite desserts, but Mom only made it for special occasions. Since Grandpa and Grandma were coming for Easter dinner, the young cook was very nervous. "What if it doesn't turn out?"

"I'll guide you along," Mom reassured her. "Crack these three eggs open, and put them into this bowl." Magdalena knew that their chicken flock hadn't been laying many eggs during the winter months. Now that the weather was getting warmer, they had enough eggs to eat for breakfast and for baking.

They mixed the rest of the ingredients into the beaten eggs all except for the flour. "The dough needs to be stiff," Mom instructed. "Put this much flour in for now. If we need more, we'll just keep adding a little at a time until it gets to the right stiffness."

Kneading was fun for Magdalena. It surprised her how fast the dry flour worked its way into the wet ingredients. When the dough was to the right consistency, Mom placed the round ball into a bowl. She covered it with a dish towel and put it into the icebox. "Why can't we fry it now?"

"It turns out better if it rests overnight," her mother answered. "Tomorrow morning the dough can be rolled out very thin and cut it into rectangles about 4 inches by 5 inches."

"I remember how you do the rest," Magdalena quickly jumped in. "Then you have to cut two lengthwise slits in each rectangle and fry them in hot oil. While they're still warm, you'll sprinkle some powdered sugar on them."

"That's right," Mom agreed, "except for one thing. I'm not going to be doing it. You're going to finish making the grebble."

Early the next morning, Magdalena fried the grebble in the hot pan of oil while Mom and her older sister Thecla (letter h is silent) began preparing some of their Easter meal. It was soon time to get dressed and head off to church.

After Mass was over, the family hurried home. Mom had plenty of work waiting for her in the kitchen. She still had to cook wurst (German sausage) and fried potatoes.

By the time Grandpa and Grandma arrived, the whole house smelled wonderful. It tasted as good as it had smelled. Mom had a way of making their holiday meals a treat. The teenager felt nervous when the sweet grebble was passed around the table. "Magdalena made it," Mom announced.

"It's very good," Grandma complimented her. "It's nice and flaky."

The young cook blushed before taking another bite of golden grebble. She had to admit it was fun to make, and it was quite tasty.

In the afternoon, the adults visited in the living room, and the kids played outside. When Magdalena came in to get a drink of water, she overheard Grandpa say, "We got a letter from Jacob." She knew that he was talking about Mom's brother. She lingered in the kitchen so she could listen in on their conversation. Grandpa continued, "He says America is the place to be. Grandma and I are too old or else it sure would be tempting to go there. It might be the answer for you young folks, though."

"Argentina was supposed to be a wonderful solution, too!" Mom retorted, "but look how it turned out for us! What if we go to America, and we don't like it?"

"You can't live your life by what ifs," Dad responded. "You just take a stab at what you think is right and go with it."

"We barely get settled in one place, and you're ready to pick up and start all over again! Once my feet are planted I'm happier staying put!" Mom emphasized her true feelings.

"I know that's what you're like, but I think it's the right thing to do," Dad argued. There was a tension in the air between her parents, and Magdalena didn't much care for it. She hurried back outside to play with her sisters and brother.

While she never heard her parents resolve their differences about moving again, they must have, because Dad left for America in the early part of the summer. He promised to send for the rest of the family as soon as he could.

One afternoon Mom told Magdalena, "Grandma wants you to come over to her house so she can measure you. She's making new dresses for you and your sisters for our trip to America."

"Can I stay over there and help her sew for a while?"

"Grandma's a very good teacher," Mom commented, "and I'm sure she'd like the company."

Magdalena ran along the dirt streets of Schuck over to her grandparents' home. Grandma had several pieces of material laid out for her to choose from. She picked one that she thought would compliment her brown hair and hazel eyes.

After measuring her, Grandma cut out the material while

Magdalena watched. "I've got four of my granddaughters' dresses done," she reported. "I haven't started your oldest sister Thecla's dress, yet." She then handed her a threaded needle and added, "I can use some help with yours."

"You must really like to sew," Magdalena remarked as she stitched two pieces of cloth together.

"It's work like anything else, but I do like sewing for special occasions," Grandma replied. "I want you girls to look your best when you step off the steamship at Ellis Island. You'll be leaving soon, and this will be my farewell gift to you."

A few days later, Magdalena walked over to Grandpa and Grandma's house and discovered her dress was completely finished. It fit her perfectly. "This is pretty!" she exclaimed. "Thank you!"

"I was hoping you'd like it," Grandma replied, sounding pleased. "You look like a beautiful young lady in it."

Not long after that, Magdalena helped Mom pack for their journey. The six dresses were neatly folded and placed into the trunk. They would remain there until the ship was about to dock in the New York harbor. "I'm looking forward to the day I can put my dress on and wear it for the first time," Magdalena expressed.

Mom never replied. She was busy putting the last items into the trunk. They were tiny cloth bags filled with garden seeds. "Our schwartzbeeren (blackberry) seeds will be over a year old before we plant them in America," her mother stated. "I wanted to take seeds from this year's bushes, but the fruit isn't ripe yet."

"Will they come up okay?" Magdalena asked.

"I think so," she answered.

"My mouth is watering for some of your blackberry dumplings," Magdalena said.

"Those do sound good," Mom agreed. "When we get

our garden established in America, you'll get your fill of them." Magdalena knew that was probably true for her mother always cooked a lot of whatever was in season.

On a nice day in August, the Hochnadel family left their home. Mom and her seven children were going to Saratov to board a train. Grandpa was in control of the horses that were pulling their wagon. They passed by a wheat field where some of their relatives were gathering the golden grain into sheaves. Grandma stopped working for a moment to wave. Magdalena took a mental picture for her memory bank. She'd seen her grandmother make a wheat sheaf many times before, but today would be the last time.

As they went on down the dirt road, Grandpa commented lovingly, "She's a strong woman. She chose not to go with us today, because her heart is breaking. Work helps get her mind off of her troubles."

"I really wish we didn't have to go our separate ways," Mom said, choking back tears.

"You've got to do what's best for your children. We're both praying that America will be a good opportunity for you," Grandpa replied. He put his arm around her and gave her a hug while holding onto the reins with his other hand.

It was a long trip into Saratov. When they arrived at the train station, Mom expressed a fear she had, "Hopefully our ship doesn't sink like the Titanic did last spring."

"You'll make it just fine," he reassured her.

All too quickly, it was time to say goodbye. "Don't forget us, Grandpa," Magdalena spoke sadly.

"You don't forget those you love," he replied simply. Ironically, she'd heard her mom say those exact words before they'd left Argentina.

"Tell Grandma I'll think of her every time I wear the dress she made for me," Magdalena requested.

"I will," he promised. His eyes were glistening before he added, "She'll like that."

They boarded the train with a destination of Liverpool, England. From there, they set sail as steerage passengers on the S. S. Adriatic, which was making its maiden voyage. On September 5, 1913, the Hochnadels stepped onto American soil. Magdalena and her five sisters were proudly wearing the beautiful dresses that Grandma's hands had lovingly sewed.

Thankfully, the immigration process never presented any problems for their family. They were healthy, and Mom must have given the right answers to their legal questions. They purchased railroad tickets and headed west to northeastern Colorado. Dad met them at the train depot. It was a joyous reunion. He was excited about their new home, and his enthusiasm rubbed off on them.

10
Settling In

The Ertle family arrived in the United States in late
fall of 1911. During the first winter, they lived in
the little town of Iliff, Colorado.

The following spring they moved to a simple, two-room
beet labor shack. The farmer they were working for provided the cramped living quarters. They spent the warm
spring days out in the field thinning his sugar beets. During the early part of summer, they did a second hoeing to
get rid of any weeds that were growing. In the fall of the
year, the family harvested his crop.

Come winter, they moved back into the town of Iliff,
Colorado, to survive the cold weather. It wasn't as harsh
as the winters of Russia, but many northeastern Colorado
days were snowy and a bite was in the air. The house in
town was nicer than the beet labor shack they lived in, but
it wasn't anything fancy. Mama never complained about
the living quarters they had in town or in the country.
Instead, she seemed content that they had a home. "Simple is good," she'd often tell Anna, her oldest daughter.

"You're always your happiest when you're satisfied with what you have."

Eleven-year-old Anna felt like her mother was a very good example. She made the most out of the inadequate houses that they were forced to live in by keeping them neat and clean. Plus, she cooked very good meals with simple ingredients. She also spent long hours out in the field, laboring alongside Papa and the rest of their family to earn their meager living.

When the Ertle children weren't helping out in the sugar beet field, they attended the Dillon School. It was a one-room country schoolhouse. In the morning as they headed out the door, Mama liked to remind Anna, "Make sure your brother and sisters get there on time."

"I always do," Anna replied before adding, "I don't like school. I'm too old for the class my teacher put me in. She made me start with the basics."

"That's because you can't speak English very well," Mama consoled her. "You'll catch on fast, because you're a smart girl."

"It's hard to learn a whole new language," Anna complained.

"Since Papa and I only speak German at home, it's probably confusing for you. In a way you're lucky, because you can go to school to learn it. Your father and I will have to slowly pick up English from you, your brothers and sisters and out in public."

Anna had never thought of herself as being able to teach her parents anything. They knew so much more than she did. "You know what the worst part about school is," she muttered. "The kids who aren't German-Russian call us Dirty Roosians, and it hurts a lot."

"Kids can be so mean!" Mama retorted quickly. "We might not have a fancy bone in our body, but we're good, honest, hard-working people. Just don't let them ever make you become ashamed of your heritage."

"I almost liked living in Russia better than I do here," Anna said, comparing the two countries. "Is that wrong?"

"No," Mama replied quickly. "Maybe you're homesick. Just remember, we've got better opportunities here than we did in the Old Country."

"Why do Americans not like us?"

"It will just take time for them to accept us," Mama gave her opinion. "You better leave for school now so you aren't late."

As Anna walked with her sisters and brother down the gravel road that led to the school grounds, her puzzled thoughts wondered, "How will I know when Americans have accepted us?"

She got her answer one afternoon when school was dismissed. It had snowed during the day. It was deep and hard to walk through, especially for the younger ones. To her surprise, a man came down the road in a nice car. He stopped and asked, "Would you like a ride? I'll be glad to give you one if you tell me where you live." He was well-dressed and had a warm, friendly smile on his face. Anna was hesitant to give him their address. The only reason she did was because her younger siblings' cheeks were rosy red from being out in the cold.

The young girl shyly climbed into his warm car and told her siblings to do the same. Their boots had snow on them. She was afraid it would melt and make his clean car dirty. Her thoughts were interrupted when the stranger introduced himself, "I'm J. P. Dillon. I'm the president of the bank here in town."

Anna thought it was rather coincidental that his last name was the same as the name of her school. "Do you own the schoolhouse?" she asked timidly.

69

"No," he chuckled. "They named the school after me, because I donated land on my ranch to build it on. I don't feel like they should have done that, but it is an honor."

The German-Russian girl was beginning to understand that he was a very important man of the community. By the time he dropped them off at their home, she also realized he was a kind American. He was the first one to extend a welcoming hand to her personally. The Ertle children saw him occasionally after that when they were walking to or from school. Whenever they did, he always stopped and offered them a ride. Anna no longer hesitated to accept his invitations.

"You're home early," Mama would say. "Did Mr. Dillon give you a lift again?"

"Yes," Anna answered. "He's a very nice man."

"He sure is," Mama agreed. "He's accepted us as Americans, and it feels good."

Not long after that, Anna had an entirely different experience while walking home from school. It was a windy day, and they were in the midst of a sandstorm. As she was being pelted by flying debris, a piece of gravel flew up, hitting her left eye. The second she walked into the house, she showed her mother. "My eye really hurts!" she exclaimed.

"It's terribly red and watery," Mama expressed her concern. "Can you see out of it?"

Anna covered her right eye with her hand. "Not very well," she replied fearfully. "I don't want to go blind."

"I don't want that, either!" Mama emphasized.

Anna knew that her parents rarely went to the doctor themselves, and they didn't take their children there very often, either. They ordered medicines by the bulk and resold it to other German-Russians in the area. Their favorite medicine was called Green Drops. It could be used for a variety of ailments. When anyone in their family had a cold, a treatment of Green Drops was in order. She wasn't sure why her mother never tried putting some of their special drops into her injured eye.

Instead, she rushed her over to the doctor's office. Unfortunately, it wasn't going to be a one-time-only office visit. He wanted to see her every day for nearly a month. Mama took her there diligently even though money was very tight. The doctor did his best, but he wasn't able to cure her problem. Eventually, she lost the sight in her left eye.

By the time Anna reached the fifth grade, the name calling by the other students had ceased. She was a young teenager now, and her parents made a decision that she should quit school and help out around the house. It didn't upset her, because she didn't see how more education would help her later on in life anyway. She could picture herself marrying a good-looking, young man. He, of course, would share her Catholic faith and German-Russian heritage. She would have lots of babies just like her mother had.

Including herself, Mama had seven children to care for. She would have had eight, but Helena had gotten very sick and died shortly after they had arrived in the United States. Anna remembered her mother's words right after it happened, "Helena's ship just docked in Heaven. She was child of God, and now she's truly reached the Promised Land."

At the time, it was hard for Anna to realize that her sister was really gone. It felt like a bad dream. That is until she saw Papa constructing a simple wood coffin to bury her in. They'd laid her to rest near the beet labor shack where they were living at the time. A few years had passed since then. They no longer worked for the same farmer, so Mama couldn't visit the grave like she yearned to do. For the most part, though, she'd buried her sorrow right along with the coffin and continued to carry on with a zest for life.

The Ertle Family in 1919.
Top row: **Anna (Suz's grandmother)**, *Glen, Joe Sr. and Myrtle.*
Bottom row: **John (Suz's great grandfather)**, *Lena, Manuel,*
Mary and **Mary Ann (Suz's great grandmother)** *holding Joe*
Jr. Note: the family lost two children, Helena and Paul. Two children
were born after photo was taken, Peter and John.

Shortly after quitting school, Anna began taking in laundry to help out with the family's expenses. Her customers
were well-to-do. They could afford to pay for the conve-
nience of having someone else do their dirty laundry.

Anna was petite for her age, and her hands were small.
She scrubbed their clothes on a washboard with all her
might. She certainly didn't want anyone to complain that
she hadn't gotten their clothes clean. She then hung them
outdoors to dry in the freshness of the wind and sunshine.
After bringing them back indoors, she stood for hours,
pressing their fancy garments with a heavy iron. She heated
the iron up on the top surface of their coal cook stove. It

was hard work, but she was used to it. After all, she'd spent many hours stooping over in the sugar beet field, thinning, hoeing or harvesting the crop.

On other days, the teenager helped Mama make homemade bread. It was something her mother had to do twice a week, every week. "We sure do eat a lot of bread," Anna commented.

"With nine mouths to feed, it takes a lot of food," Mama replied. "Why I've been baking eight loaves at a time for quite a while now. I can't even imagine what it would be like to make only one loaf."

"The house always smells so good when the bread is baking," Anna complimented her.

Bread was one of Anna's favorite foods, especially when it had a filling inside it. Mama made the best schwartzbeeren (blackberry) strudel. After rolling out the dough, she spread the fruit that had been mixed with flour and sugar on top of it. She then carefully drew up the sides and ends and pinched them shut. As the dessert baked, it made their home smell homey.

Anna and her siblings got the job of picking the blackberries. It was one task that never felt like work. It was as if she was going outdoors on a picnic. She could eat all the tiny fruit she wanted, soak up some warm sunshine and enjoy nature.

It had taken time, but she'd come to the conclusion that America really was a good place to live.

11
Sugar Beet Harvest

B y the fall of 1914, Johannes Gartner had been in the United States for two years. The seventeen-year-old began noticing that American males with the same first name as his were known as John. He liked the American version, and he began going by it.

Even though WWI was causing global unrest, it seemed like a world away to John. He spent his days out in the sugar beet field, working alongside his family. They labored from sunrise to sunset. He was strong for his age, and his father depended upon him and his older brother Joe to handle a variety of jobs. They could do the pulling, topping and loading of the crop.

The first process of harvest was done by the farmer they worked for. He operated the beet puller, which was drawn by three workhorses. He sat on a nice seat as the horses went up and down the field. The beet puller had two knives, which passed along the sides of a row. The sharp blades loosened the soil but did not pull the large roots out of the ground. It was up to the German-Russian laborers to finish the process.

Most days the Gartners never even saw the farmer. He was off doing something else. It was as if their family was isolated from the rest of society. So when an expensive vehicle pulled up beside the field and parked, it captivated the whole family's attention. "Wonder who that is," Dad remarked suspiciously. A middle-aged man soon got out of the car. He was neatly dressed and was carrying a camera. As he began walking across the field, it appeared as if he was trying very hard not to get his shoes dirty. John glanced down at his overalls, which were covered with smears of dry dirt. "If he wants to take pictures of people looking their best, he's come to the wrong place," he said before snickering.

The uninvited visitor stepped up to Dad and introduced himself before informing him, "I'm here to take a few photos for the National Child Labor Committee. They've sent me to northeastern Colorado to get pictures of children helping with the sugar beet harvest. In other parts of the country, I've taken snapshots of children working in textile mills, canneries and sweatshops."

John wasn't certain why the stranger cared if he and his siblings were working out in the field, but he could tell by the look in his father's dark eyes that he wanted to kick the intruder out of the field right then and there. He couldn't do it, because it wasn't his land. He had no right to do so. The photographer took several pictures of the twins Anna and Alex as they were stooped over pulling up beets. They were young, but they could still help out in the field. John felt self-conscious when it was his turn to pose in front of the camera. After each photo was snapped, the well-groomed man asked their ages and names. He wrote the information down in a notebook.

When the photographer was finished with his assignment, he gave his opinion, "This kind of work is too hard and dangerous for your kids to be doing. One of these days this kind of lifestyle will not be socially acceptable. Your youngsters should be in school learning."

John saw his father's face get red with anger. He knew the outspoken stranger was treading on thin ice. "Don't you understand that we rely upon whole families to get this kind of work done?" Dad replied curtly. "It takes 55 to 60 hours of manual labor to harvest just one acre, and this is a twenty-acre field."

"I'm just doing what my boss told me to do. I'm documenting underage children who are working in agriculture. People above me are the ones that have the power to change things if they so choose," the educated man spoke smugly before gingerly stepping his way back across the field.

As soon as the sophisticated photographer was out of hearing distance, John's younger sister Lizzie exclaimed, "I hope he gets his shiny, black shoes all dirty!"

The rest of the family all laughed at her comment except for Dad. Clearly, he was still hot under the collar. "Those city people don't have a clue what it takes to make a living out here. The more helping hands you have, the faster the work gets done. They seem to think that you can learn everything you'll ever need to know out of books."

John didn't understand what all the fuss was about. When he wasn't busy helping out in the field, he'd gone to school and learned how to read and write. He knew plenty enough to get by. True, it was hard work out in the field, but he never minded the feel of dirt on his hands. He'd much rather spend the day outdoors than be stuck indoors at school.

Obviously, the intruder's distraction had interrupted their work long enough. "Daylight's a burnin'!" Dad stressed. Everyone knew that meant it was time to get back to their jobs.

Anna, Alex, Lizzie and Pauline once again stooped over to pull the cumbersome, cream-colored roots out of the loosened soil and lay them in a row. Dad, Mom and George got busy topping the sugar beets. They used the curved hook of their topping knives to pick them up. With a swift motion of the sharp blade, they chopped off the green, leafy tops. The pulpy beets were then tossed into the shallow ditch, forming a pile. Every so often, a new pile would be started.

Meanwhile, John and his older brother Joe walked back to where four workhorses were patiently standing. They were hitched to the wagon two abreast.

John shoved his gloved hand through the handle of his wide beet fork. He heaved the heavy beets of varying sizes and shapes over the sideboard of the wagon, one forkful at a time. On average, the beets weighed between two and five pounds each and were six to ten inches long.

When the wagon was piled high, Dad took the heavy load to the nearest beet dump. It was located about three miles from the farm near the town of Iliff, Colorado. The receiving station accepted beets from all the farmers in the nearby vicinity.

The two brothers then went to help Mom and George top the beets. As John worked, he recalled the time he had accompanied his father to the beet dump. It was quite an experience. He was amazed at how busy the place was. A string of wagons were waiting in line. When it was their turn to be weighed, Dad stopped the team beside a small building. A man was inside operating a balance beam scale. He shouted the total weight of their wagon through an open window. It was just over 4 tons.

Dad then proceeded forward and pulled up behind the

wagon at the end of the line. When it was time to advance, the double-teamed horses were raring to go. They pulled the heavily loaded wagon up the wooden ramp. It had a long, gentle incline. Just as soon as they reached the highest point where it leveled out, Dad yelled, "Whoa!"

John glanced down at the partially filled railroad car parked below. Dad got off and unhooked the front and back sides of the wing. A few sugar beets began rolling down the tilted platform. Meanwhile, an employee of the receiving station put a hook on the other side of the wagon. The box was tilted on its side. Gravity took over, and the tumbling beets caused quite a commotion. It didn't take long for the last ones to roll off. The worker then lowered the wagon's box, and Dad hooked the wing back in place. They headed down the wooden ramp that had a gradual decline. Once again, they stopped at the scale house. This time it was to get an empty weight.

On the way back to the farm, John asked, "How do the beets get to the sugar factory?"

"When they get enough full rail cars, a train engine pulls them to Sterling," Dad explained. "It's nice that there's a factory located only 13 miles from us. That's where they process the beets into sugar. It keeps our family working. Don't know how we'd earn a living without this kind of work."

He came back to reality when his older brother Joe shouted at him in a kidding manner, "Quit your daydreaming! We've got work to do!" John hadn't realized that he was standing there, staring off into space.

When their father returned to the field, John could tell he was in a hurry. "I'll help you boys load. If we hustle, we can get another one to the dump before they close today." The extra help made the job go a lot faster. Soon they had the wagon filled to capacity and almost bursting at the seams. Dad coaxed the workhorses to pull it out of the field.

The family of nine knew they would be working out in the field six days a week until the crop was completely harvested. On Sundays, they went to church and rested.

During the week, John looked forward to their mid-morning and mid-afternoon breaks. The family gathered around while Mom sliced their homemade sour watermelons. Whenever she worked out in the field she wore a scarf. Strands of her long dark hair fell below it.

"Sour watermelons sure do hit the spot when you're hungry and thirsty," John remarked after taking a big bite out of his slice. Pink juice was dripping off his chin. He only paused with his chewing when he had to spit out the small, black seeds.

"I'm glad that we brought watermelon seeds with us from Russia," Mom stated. "I've tried pickling other varieties, but these small ones that have a hard, pale green rind sour the best. I think it's because the pulp stays pink and firm even though they're fully ripe."

"Do people in America eat sour watermelons?" nine-year-old Lizzie asked.

"No," Mom answered. "They're part of our German-Russian culture."

"How long does it take for them to get sour?" she inquired.

"About two weeks," Mom replied.

Dad then directed the flow of conversation in a more serious direction by saying, "I think it's high time that we change our last name. Ever since we've been in America, it has caused us nothing but problems. There's paperwork for everything here. Russia wasn't that way. There are a lot of Gartners in our area and some have the same first name, which causes us more trouble than its worth."

"What would we change it to?" Mom asked.

"We could change the a to an e. Then our last name

The Gertner Family in 1917.
Top row: *Joseph Jr., Pauline, Lizzie and* **John (Suz's grandfather.)** Bottom row: **Joseph Sr.** **(Suz's great grandfather***),*
Anna, **Mary (Suz's great grandmother),** *Alex and George.*
Note: the family lost two children, Peter and Jacob.

would be Gertner," he answered. "I like the sounds of that."

"So do I," Mom agreed.

"Then it's settled," Dad concluded. "We'll make the change." He tossed his watermelon rind on the ground and walked back to where they'd been harvesting. The rest of the family knew that was their cue to get back to work.

That fall, they finished harvesting earlier than the Ertle family did. Dad offered to help them out, because the weather was getting colder by the day. John didn't mind one bit. Their oldest daughter Anna was just four years younger than he was. Her family lived right across the street from his when they lived in Russia. He hadn't paid

81

much attention to her then, but she had really grown up since those days.

As they worked at separate tasks out in the beet field, he couldn't put his finger on it, but he knew there was something special about her. There were a lot of German-Russian girls living in the area, but he felt more self-conscious around her than the others. He really wanted to make a good impression. The trouble was she made him so nervous that he barely spoke a word to her. No matter how buried in work he was, he always knew exactly where she was in the field. Dad must have noticed, because he kidded, "Kind of sweet on Anna, are you?"

"Maybe a little," John replied. He felt his face flush red, and it wasn't from the cold temperature of the outdoors.

12
Rooshun Corner

When the Hochnadels first arrived in America in 1913, they had no choice but to live with Magdalena's Uncle Jacob and his family. With so many people residing in the small house, it was crowded. Fourteen-year-old Magdalena longed for a house they could call their own.

Since Uncle Jacob had been in America for a while, he was able to help them adjust to living in the United States. Things were done much different here than in the Old Country. Thanks to him, their family found work laboring in sugar beet fields. In the off-season, Magdalena's father had gotten a good job working for the railroad. Little by little, they were able to save up some money.

It was a wonderful day when their family purchased a tiny, three-room house on Douglas Street in Sterling, Colorado. The wood-frame house had an attached porch, and a picket fence surrounded the property. They'd barely set

The Hochnadel Family about 1918.

Top row: *Elizabeth,* **Magdalena (Suz's grandmother)**, *Barbara and Katherine.* Middle row: **John (Suz's great grandfather)**, *Mary,* **Anna Maria (Suz's great grandmother)** *and Magdalena's Uncle Jacob.* Bottom row: *Rose, Annie on mother's lap, Andrew and John. Note: Thecla, oldest daughter, is not pictured. The family lost one child, Phillip. Joe was born after photo was taken.*

foot in the backyard, and Mom was already making plans for the future. "I can plant a small garden over there, and I already know what I want to do with that small, old building. I'll turn it into a chicken house. We'll have all the fresh eggs we can eat."

The house certainly wasn't anything fancy, but it was new to them. It was located in the section of town where only German-Russian families lived. They were surrounded by neighbors who thought and acted very much like they did. "It feels like we're living in the village of Schuck again," Magdalena commented.

"Not quite," Mom answered. "You've heard the towns-people say that we live in the Rooshun Corner, haven't you?"

"Yes, why do they call it that?"

"They're putting us down," Mom replied. "They don't know that we proudly call our little corner of the town Russe Ecke. As long as we like where we live, it doesn't matter what they say about it."

Magdalena knew her mother's thinking was correct, but the nickname still bothered her. Whenever she crossed over into the main portion of the town, she could tell that the local residents were shunning her. She didn't like the feeling. She gradually realized that her people weren't trying very hard to be accepted, either. They dressed different than the Americans did and held onto many of the customs they'd brought over from Russia. It was as if they were afraid to lose their old ways.

Time didn't improve the situation. Local residents continued to refer to the section of town she lived in as the "Rooshun Corner."

On a January afternoon in 1917, Magdalena was at home with her sisters and brothers. Her parents had gone to the Great Western Sugar Factory, which was located on the opposite side of town. She was hungry so she opened a jar of Mom's preserved schwartzbeeren (blackberry) jelly. She thought it would taste good on a slice of home-made bread. She used her right hand to twist off the lid. As she did so, she noticed her crooked index finger. She'd injured it several years ago, and her parents hadn't taken her to the doctor. The finger was normal up to the knuckle, but it curved sharply upward and got much smaller near the tip. Fortunately, it wasn't a handicap to her. It was just the looks of the deformed finger that bothered her. "I can understand why strangers stare at it," she was thinking when her thoughts were interrupted.

"Ah-ver!" her ten-year-old sister Barbara exclaimed as she sauntered into the kitchen. The word was a spin-off from their native German language. It was just as powerful as if she would have extended her index finger on one hand and rubbed the other index finger across it while she scolded, "Shame, shame! You know better than that! You're going to be in trouble with Mom!"

Magdalena knew her sister was probably right, but the jar was already open. She spread the thin purple jelly on a slice of bread and proceeded to take a bite.

It was soon evident that Barbara's scolding was over. She was busy making herself a snack, too. "Mmm...this tastes good in the middle of winter," she expressed her opinion. As she went to take another bite, some jelly fell onto the front of her dress.

This time it was Magdalena's turn to say, "Ah-ver! That's going to be hard to get out."

Barbara tried washing it off, but she wasn't doing a very good job of it. Then, the big sister in Magdalena took over. She scrubbed on it harder and got most of the stain to disappear.

When their parents got home, they weren't concerned about the partially eaten jar of blackberry jelly. Magdalena instantly knew that there was a tension between them. Dad was holding some papers in his hand. Mom summed up what was bothering her, "He wants to move again. First we went to South America, then back to Russia and then to here."

"Where are we going to move to?" Magdalena asked.

"Missoula, Montana," Dad replied. "The Great Western Sugar Factory has a promotion going on. They're trying to recruit German-Russians from this area to move to Montana. They've heard that we're very hard workers. I'd like to check out the deal they're offering."

Mom threw her hands up in the air. She knew it was use-
less to argue for his mind was already made up. He had the
notion that moving to Montana would become the opportunity he needed to own land someday.

Magdalena didn't like being uprooted again, but
their family was in the process of doing just that. Before
long, they found themselves living out in the country
near the city of Missoula. There were two rivers and five
mountain ranges nearby. Even though the mountains
were pretty, she still preferred the flat plains of northeastern Colorado.

The land on which they were to raise sugar beets had
been plowed the previous fall. This was going to be the first
crop of sugar beets grown there. In late April, they planted
the seeds and waited for them to come up.

On the first day of May, Magdalena turned 18. To make
her birthday special, Mom asked, "What would you like
me to bake for you?"

"Pumpernickel bread," she replied. "It's my favorite."

Since Mom traditionally only made the German bread
on New Year's Day, it was considered a dessert around
their household. As it baked, the kitchen smelled wonderful, making Magdalena hungrier than usual.

She was glad when noon arrived. Right after everyone finished silently praying their before meal prayers,
they sang, "Happy Birthday" to her in German. It didn't
seem possible to Magdalena that she was eighteen-years-
old. A lot of the German-Russian girls who were her age
or younger were already married. She didn't know how
many more birthdays she'd celebrate while still living at
home. So she was thoroughly enjoying the special attention this one was bringing her. She bit into a piece of the
dark, coarse bread. It had a heavy texture and was slightly
sweet. "The bread's really good," she complimented her

mother. In fact, it was down right delicious. After finishing her first piece, she couldn't resist slicing off another one. Meanwhile, everyone but Mom was finished eating. They got up and left.

"One of these days you'll make pumpernickel bread for your family, too," Mom predicated.

"Me, get married!" Magdalena exclaimed. "To who?"

"That's for you to decide," Mom replied as she got up and began clearing off the kitchen table.

Later that month, the family began thinning out the extra sugar beets. The long hours out in the field, going up and down rows, gave Magdalena a lot of thinking time. She loved to reflect back upon the days she'd lived in Russia. She knew the government hadn't made life easy for the adults who called Schuck home, but she had been a carefree child there. She wondered if the village had changed much since they left. She remembered the special dress Grandma had sewed for her as a farewell gift. She missed her grandparents and hoped they were getting along fine.

A few weeks after the thinning was completed, it was time to do the second hoeing. They chopped out weeds that were missed the first time or new ones that had cropped up since then.

By mid-summer, Magdalena noticed how quiet and dejected her father seemed. Discouragement was showing in his eyes.

In September, Dad picked up a shovel and asked the family to join him. He walked at a quick pace out to the edge of the field. Magdalena wondered what he was planning on doing. He dug up a root with his shovel. Compared to the beets she'd helped harvest back in Colorado, it was small and spindly. "We've done our best to care for the crop, but these beets aren't going to amount to anything. It's no use. All we're doing is wasting our time," he spoke seriously before throwing down his shovel. His words had a powerful sting to them, and silence fell over the field.

It was soon evident that Mom's spirit wasn't broken like Dad's was. She quickly suggested, "If we leave now, we can be back in Sterling, Colorado, before harvest starts. Farmers in the area know our work ethic. Someone will hire us."

Dad didn't argue. He must have thought it was the only sensible thing to do. He looked directly into Mom's eyes and apologized, "I should have listened to you in the first place. You were right, and I was wrong. I'm sorry for dragging this family through another ordeal. Once we get back to northeastern Colorado, I'll never get a wild notion to move to another state or country ever again. That is where we'll live out the rest of our lives."

Magdalena felt sorry for Dad. He looked so disheartened. She felt a sense of relief when Mom smiled and threw her arms around his neck, giving him a big hug. Almost instantly, he squared his shoulders just like the world had been lifted off of them. "I know you better than you know yourself," she said gently. "You'll always have the itch to move. It will be okay with me as long as we stay in Colorado. I like that state, and we have relatives living there."

As the family of eleven traveled back to Sterling, they knew what lay ahead for them. They would be laboring from sunrise to sunset, harvesting sugar beets. That is all except for Mom. It was obvious that she would be having another baby soon. Magdalena recalled the terrible day when her infant brother died right after birth, and Dad had to bury him at sea on their journey to Argentina. She certainly hoped this baby would be healthy for her mother's sake.

In October, the Hochnadels were overjoyed with the addition of another girl. They named her Annie.

Dad had to work extra hard that fall without Mom's help out in the field. He didn't seem to mind one bit. The wages they received enabled them to move back to Russe Ecke as they lovingly called it. They didn't care if the townspeople referred to it as the Rooshun Corner. For them, it was home sweet home.

13
Registering for the Draft

After settling down in Ovid, Colorado in 1913, the Lambrecht family earned their living by working for a farmer. Season after season, they toiled in his fields under all kinds of weather conditions.

Pete, who was the oldest son of the family, was like his father's right hand man. All that might be changing, though. The end of WWI was not in sight. Millions of men were already fighting overseas, because they'd volunteered or been drafted. More men were needed in the military.

When Pete woke up at dawn on June 5, 1918, he had an uneasy feeling. He was 22, and it was mandatory for him to register that day. Local draft boards were set up in every county across the nation. He would have to travel into Sedgwick, the county seat, which was eight miles away.

By the time Pete had gotten dressed in his church clothes and walked into the kitchen, the rest of the family was already gathered there. Mom was bustling about putting

The Lambrecht Family about 1926.
Top row: *Catherine,* **Pete (Suz's grandfather)**, *Joseph, George Jr. and August.* Bottom row: **Kaderina (Suz's great grandmother)**, *Mary and* **George Sr. (Suz's great grandfather.)**
Note: Rose, oldest daughter, is not pictured.

the finishing touches on their breakfast. When she saw him, her eyes expressed worry. "I just don't see why you have to register," she fretted. "You're not even a U. S. citizen. I wouldn't even go do it."

"I have to!" Pete emphasized. "If I don't register, I'll be considered a draft dodger."

"That's true," Dad joined in on the conversation. "If the military calls him, it'll be his duty to go. At least, Russia's on America's side. What I don't like is you'd be fighting against the Germans. Our bloodlines go back there. Even though our ancestors left Germany in the late 1700s, we probably still have relatives living in the country."

"Just because I sign up doesn't mean I'd be shipped overseas," Pete tried to calm the tension in the air. "They have deferments for those involved with farming."

"I know that," Mom stated. "What I don't like is how Americans are treating us since this war's been going on. German-Russians can't even gather on street corners and talk. They break us up, because they think we're plotting something. It makes me feel like a criminal, and I haven't done anything wrong. And you're supposed to put your life on the line for a country like that!"

Tears welled up in her eyes. Dad walked over and gave her a soothing hug. "War scares everyone, but it'll be okay," he said, trying to reassure her.

Those few words helped Mom to compose herself. They also gave Pete some peace of mind.

Right after breakfast, he saddled up Lightning. The farmer they worked for was letting him borrow his saddle horse for the day. His parents had come out to the yard and were standing side-by-side. "If we didn't have so much work to do, we'd go into town with you to show our support," Dad explained.

"That's okay," Pete answered. "I understand." He was grateful that he had such wonderful parents. He knew they were very close. The farmer they worked for had also noticed. He'd recently told him, "Where one is, you'll find the other."

Pete kicked his heels into Lightning's sides and waved goodbye. It was a gorgeous morning. The sun was shining and only a few white, puffy clouds broke up the deep blue sky. There was a slight breeze to stir the air. It made for a pleasant ride into town.

As Pete rode along Main Street, he was surprised. It looked like everyone in the county had come into town to celebrate. All the businesses were closed, and it wasn't a holiday. He soon realized the town was showing their support for the draft registration. It was a festive occasion, and patriotism filled the air. Even though it was Wednesday, he heard church bells ringing. He loved the sound of their chiming. Shortly after that a train's whistle blew. It was a lonesome but comforting sound.

Pete made his way over to the courthouse and tied Lightning up to a nearby pole. He joined the long line of young men, who were waiting to be registered for the draft. At that moment, it hit him. He truly was doing the honorable thing.

While he waited his turn, he had time to think about what it would mean to travel overseas and fight. He remembered all too well how terrible the conditions on the steamship were when they had immigrated to the United States. He was getting queasy just thinking about rough ocean waters. He was further troubled by the thought, "Can I kill another human being even if he is an enemy?"

The line moved rather quickly, and he soon found himself at the front of it. A distinguished-looking man with a neatly trimmed moustache was seated behind a desk. Pete could read and write simple words in English, but it was a challenge for him. The older gentleman asked him a series of questions and filled out the paperwork based upon his answers. He was relieved that he only had to sign the registration card. The registrar then stamped it and stated, "You're a Class 5."

"What does that mean?"

"You won't be subject for induction," he replied. "I assigned that class to you, because you're an alien resident and the oldest son of a farm family."

"I want to make sure I understand," Pete said. "I won't be drafted no matter how long the war goes on."

"That is correct," the registrar answered. Then he looked at the young man behind Pete and motioned him forward.

By the time Pete got home, it was suppertime. When everyone was gathered around the table, he shared his news. "I was hoping you wouldn't have to serve," Dad reacted with relief. "Earning a living the way we do takes a lot of hands."

That summer and fall, Pete was kept very busy with the farm work. He and his father did the hardest, heaviest labor. His mother, sisters and younger brothers did the easier tasks.

On November 11, 1918, welcome news spread across the entire country. WW1 was over!

The following winter, Pete married Magdalena Herschfeld. Like him, she was a German-Russian immigrant so they had a lot in common.

A few months down the road, the couple announced to their families that they were expecting their first child. Pete was looking forward to being a father. Everything went well throughout the pregnancy.

When the labor pains came, he rushed over to the neighbor's house to fetch the midwife. She would be delivering their baby. The older woman immediately dropped what she was doing and rushed out the door with Pete.

It was a long night for the expectant father. He'd never been through this before so he had no idea what to expect. His thoughts were swirling about aimlessly. One minute he was excited, wondering if the newborn child would be a boy or girl. The next minute, he was worried about his wife. He'd only spent a few moments in the bedroom with her, but it was enough to see the pain she was going through. Anguish was written all over her young face. As he sat at the kitchen table, all he could feel was helplessness. There simply wasn't anything he could do to ease her pain.

Hours later, the bedroom door opened and a solemn midwife emerged. He was confused. Why did she look so sad, and why wasn't he hearing a baby's cry? Silence filled the house until she spoke softly, "I'm sorry, Pete. It was a difficult childbirth. Both the baby and your wife didn't make it."

He'd heard the words spoken by the neighbor woman, but they were hard to comprehend. Instead of having an addition to the family, he was a young widower.

"I'll go tell Magdalena's family and yours the heart-breaking news," she spoke compassionately.

For a while after the burial, Pete felt like his wife would come back at any second, and everything would be normal again. It didn't happen for she and their child had gone to Heaven to be with Jesus. That gave him comfort, but life had lost its meaning without her by his side.

Time didn't come to a halt just because he was grieving. It continued to click slowly away, healing his wounds. Through the trying ordeal, Pete's faith had grown stronger.

Eventually, he was ready to start over. Ironically, the next woman he chose to marry was also named Magdalena—Magdalena Hochnadel that is. They had grown up in Russian villages just five miles apart, but they didn't know one another in the Old Country.

Because they were young teenagers when they immigrated to the United States with their families, they remembered the wedding customs that were observed back in Russia. It was a tradition for the young couple to choose two men to be their representatives, who went into the Volga River Valley to invite guests to their marriage ceremony. These men carried with them a cane that the bride-to-be had tied a ribbon on. At each household, they recited a poem, which was really an invitation to the wedding. If the family tied a ribbon on the cane, it meant they were accepting the invitation.

Since the Volga Germans had been in the United States for several years now, a lot of the engaged couples had dropped that tradition. The news of an upcoming wedding quickly spread throughout their community. Weddings were looked forward to and eagerly attended.

When Magdalena and Pete sat down to decide on their wedding date, they didn't even think about breaking several old-time traditions. The ceremony must be held in the wintertime, on a weekday and not during Lent. They'd never been to a wedding that wasn't held in the months of January, February or March. It was much easier to take time out for celebrations in the winter months, because farm work was at its slowest season and there was ample time to prepare for it. Come springtime, it would mean long, busy hours back out in the fields.

After deciding on a date of Monday, February 7, 1921, Pete asked, "Do you want to have a Dutch Hop after the wedding?"

"I don't see why not," Magdalena replied. "It's a tradition our ancestors started, and everyone loves dancing to the music played by a polka band."

On the day of the wedding, Pete tucked a flower in his left lapel and pinned a long, wide ribbon under it. The light-colored sash draped down the entire length of his dark suit coat. He looked like a typical German-Russian groom.

After the ceremony at St. Anthony's Catholic Church, the newlyweds rode in a decorated wagon pulled by well-groomed horses. They were on their way to take their wedding picture at the only studio in Sterling, Colorado.

The photographer was already set up. It was standard practice for the groom to be seated in a chair so Pete sat down. His bride stood beside him on his left side.

She put her white-gloved right hand on his shoulder. In her left hand, Magdalena held a bouquet of flowers. Her wedding dress was all white and came to mid calf. A veil adorned her head and flowed just below her dress length. Pointed, button-up high heel shoes rounded out her attire.

Just before the photographer was ready to click the camera, Pete whispered, "How you doing, Mrs. Lambrecht?"

The new last name sounded foreign to Magdalena. "Happy to be your wife," she replied softly. She paused slightly before adding, "and ready for the picture taking to be over."

"Better hope we take a good one," he laughed. "It'll be a keepsake passed onto future generations."

Both the bride and groom refrained from smiling too much when the photo was taken. It wasn't fashionable to be all smiles in the 1920s even if ones heart was filled with joy.

Pete Lambrecht and Magdalena Hochnadel's
wedding photo, February 7, 1921.
The bride and groom were teenagers when they immigrated to Amer-ica. The groom has a sash pinned to his lapel. He is carrying on a German-Russian custom.

14
Worldwide
Flu of 1918

During WWI, the Spanish Flu became a pandemic. Millions around the globe were dying from the disease with pneumonia being the primary cause of death. Ironically, the flu was causing more casualties than the war. The virus was a very unusual strain that baffled doctors, because it claimed the young and healthy for victims rather than the old and weak. There was no cure for it. Those who came down with the virus had to fight it on their own, and they either quickly won or swiftly lost the battle.

The flu spread along the east coast at an alarming rate. An urgent warning was sent to the rest of the country to start making coffins and digging graves and for good reason. It was as if the elusive virus purchased a railroad ticket and followed the rails out west.

At the time, John Gertner was 21 and Anna Ertle was 16. For them, life was carefree and more wonderful than it had ever been. Their love was in the blooming process.

"Do you want to attend a wedding with me and my family on Saturday afternoon?" he asked.

"Who's getting married?"

"Ralph," John replied. "He's the son of the farmer my family works for."

"I would like that."

"We'll be over to pick you up around one o'clock," he confirmed the date.

Saturday afternoon soon arrived. On the way to the wedding, Anna sat next to John in the back seat of their car. Since her family never owned an automobile, she really enjoyed how fast it traveled. It seemed like the 13-mile trip into town was over almost before it began.

Anna thought it was a lovely ceremony, but it wasn't like any she had ever attended before. The service was much shorter than German-Russian weddings were.

When the Gertners dropped Anna off at her house, John walked her to the door. "I feel kind of funny. I just don't feel right," she told him.

Alarm overpowered his tender blue eyes, "I hope you're not coming down with the Spanish Flu."

"I'll be fine," she responded quickly. "It's probably nothing."

That night, she went to bed earlier than usual. Her fever soared, and fear welled up inside her. She didn't have a doubt in her mind that she had the dreaded virus.

Meanwhile, John's mother suddenly came down with the life-threatening flu. He was terribly worried about her even though he knew she was a strong, hard-working lady. Always in the past she had said, "Even if I'm sick, I've got to keep on going." And that's exactly what she did. This illness was different, though. She stayed in bed and never even attempted to care for her family. It didn't take long for the virus to claim her life.

To stop the spread of the flu, public places were closed down. Schools weren't in session and church services were cancelled. People were ordered to stay at home if they were sick.

It was almost a month before John and Anna saw each again. Without even saying a word, they both knew the other one had been terribly sick. John sadly informed her of his mother's death. "I'm so sorry," she said compassionately.

"I know you are," he replied. "How are you feeling?"

She could sense that he didn't want to talk anymore about his late mother so she responded to his question, "Some of my hair fell out. I think it was because of the high fever." Without thinking, she ran her fingers through the light brown strands before continuing, "When I could start eating again, onions were the only thing that tasted good. They had a sweet flavor, and everything else tasted bitter."

"I'm sorry you had to go through all that," he replied. "I feel like it was my fault. If you hadn't come to the wedding with us, you might not have gotten sick."

"The flu was everywhere," she commented quietly. "There was no safe place to hide from it. I heard my younger sisters playing jump rope the other day. As they skipped over it, they chanted: I had a little bird, its name was Enza. I opened up the window and in flew Enza."

Anna was glad when John opened up to her about his ordeal with the flu. "I was so sick that Dad decided to drive me into town for medical help," he said. "I stayed at a house that was turned into a makeshift hospital. Several times a day, the doctor came to check on me and the others."

"Was there a lot of patients?"

"Yes," John replied. "After the doctor released me, I walked over to my aunt's house. I was hungry for a sour watermelon, and I knew she'd have some. It was delicious! I soon began to feel much better, and I thought maybe the sour watermelons would help the other patients. So I took some back to the hospital, but the doctor didn't think it would be a good idea."

"I'm glad you're better," she said. Sincerity shone forth from her blue eyes.

"Me, too," John replied. "I'm going into town tomorrow and visit Mom's grave. Since I was sick, I wasn't able to be there when the family buried her."

Early the next morning, John went into Sterling. He drove along a winding road through Riverside Cemetery. He never had any trouble finding his mother's grave, because his family told him where she was buried. The headstone had a big cross on top of it. His mom's name, Mary Gertner, was etched in stone followed simply with, "Died Aug. 11, 1918." The grass in front of it hadn't recuperated from being disturbed recently. He sadly walked down a lengthy row of markers. One after another's date of death was 1918. He didn't recognize any of the names, but he knew the same virus that had claimed his loved one's life most likely had taken theirs as well. Some of the victims were babies or toddlers. All of a sudden, his thoughts turned toward his younger sister Lizzie. Since she was the oldest girl in the family, the huge responsibility of cooking, cleaning and caring for her younger siblings naturally fell upon her shoulders. She was doing her best to fill Mom's shoes, but a void still plagued their household.

John lingered a while longer before touching his mom's tombstone lightly. There was nothing more he could do at the cemetery, and there was work to be done at the farm. As he drove home, his thoughts focused on Dad. Right after Mom had passed away, he'd sent a letter to her parents in Russia, informing them of the bad news. The letter was returned a few days later. His father had marched into the post office to find out the reason why. That evening at supper, he was still steaming mad, "This is ridiculous!" he exclaimed. "German-Russians are forbidden to send letters back to their relatives in Russia, and we can't receive them either because of the war!"

"That'll make us lose all contact with our relatives in the Old Country," John spoke up.

"That's exactly right!" Dad's tone remained harsh. "The sting of being an immigrant is still with us…maybe always will be. Our only choice is to carry on with our daily lives the best we can."

Several weeks later, it was time to harvest sugar beets. John was still weak from his battle with the flu, but he didn't even think about not doing his fair share of hard, physical labor. Dad needed his help, and he wouldn't let him down.

A year later, John asked Anna to be his wife. She agreed but wasn't sold on the idea of having a Dutch Hop (wedding dance.) "It'll cost too much money," she fretted.

"Don't you worry about that," John said smiling. "I've been saving up money for it. I've got $300, which should be enough to cover the expenses."

"In that case, I suppose it'll be okay," Anna concluded.

In keeping with German-Russian tradition, a winter wedding was planned. During the two-day celebration, they would need an abundance of food to feed their many guests. A few days before the wedding was scheduled to take place, a group of ladies got together and made homemade noodles and butchered old laying hens.

Several ladies volunteered to finish preparing the big meal while the wedding was taking place. They were kept busy cooking the noodle soup and other traditional main dishes. One of the desserts they would be serving was Rivel Kuga (bread topped with a layer of schwartzbeeren (blackberries) with a crumbly mixture of flour, sugar and lard sprinkled over the fruit.)

John Gertner and Anna Ertle were wed in holy matrimony at St. Anthony's Catholic Church on February 16, 1920. And the two became one.

After taking their wedding photos at a studio, it was time for them to go the hall where their Dutch Hop was being held. Petite Anna was wearing her tiny, white wedding dress that came to mid calf. She pinned a handkerchief onto her beautiful dress. It was customary for anyone wishing to dance with the bride to pin money onto her handkerchief before doing so. After each dance was over, Anna carefully removed the money and put it into a box for safekeeping.

Guests sat on chairs, which were lined up around the sides of the hall. Band members played a variety of music including, "The Bride and Groom Waltz and Wedding Day Polka." They sang during some of the songs in their familiar German language.

Everyone, including the young and old, could participate in a Dutch Hop. Dancers divided up into pairs or even trios. A common way to dance was side-by-side with their arms wrapped around their partner's waist. Dancing styles varied from hops, kicks, sideways steps, shuffles, bounces or just walking forward.

Regardless of the tempo or rhythm of the music, dancers could use the same step. Sometimes when a song was winding down, the musicians played a strong beat followed by three thumps. Meanwhile, dancers had fun stomping their feet on the wooden floor. The celebration wound down at midnight.

At six o'clock the following morning, the second and final day of festivities were about to recommence. "I don't know if my feet will hold up to another day of dancing," Anna fretted.

"It'll be easier than working out in the beet field all day," John replied jokingly.

"That's true," she admitted readily. The newlyweds walked hand-in-hand to the middle of the large room. It was customary for them to be the center of attention for the first dance of the day. When it was over, Anna danced with whoever asked her and John found a partner, as well.

During one of their breaks, the couple opened their wedding gifts. They had only received three presents. The farmer that John and his family worked for gave them a nice set of dishes. "Those are going to come in handy," the groom commented.

As luck would have it, the other gift boxes both contained white bedspreads. Anna knew that she would use the plain, less expensive one right away, because that was the practical thing to do. The other bedspread was very pretty and obviously quite expensive. She would store it away.

When the celebration ended and the money was tallied up, it wasn't quite enough to cover their expenses. There were no regrets, though. John and Anna had made memories that would last a lifetime.

15
First
American
Generation of
Lambrechts

A few months before the stock market crash occurred in 1929, Pete and Magdalena Lambrecht welcomed a fifth child into their family. They named their daughter Florence.

By the time she was six, her father had worked his way up from being a laborer in sugar beet fields to farming rented land near Padroni, Colorado. It was difficult for the family to make a living off of the land during the Great Depression and Dust Bowl years, because crop prices were low. Consequently, the young girl with brunette hair and dark brown eyes grew up in tough times without knowing the difference. From her parents' example, Florence was learning how to be frugal, just as they had from theirs.

German was the principal language spoken at home by her parents. As a result, when Florence started first grade at the country school in Padroni, she could speak wonderful German. The only trouble was her English wasn't very good. The little she knew had been picked up from her older brothers and sister.

There were only four teachers for eight grades. Each of the instructors had been assigned two classes. Her teacher was responsible for both the first and second grade students.

At the end of the school year, Florence's teacher told her something she didn't want to hear. "I'm sorry, but you won't be moving up to the second grade. It's because of the language barrier you've had to overcome. Your English has improved a lot throughout this school year, and next year will be easy for you."

The teacher was right. Each school year seemed to get a little easier for her. Before she knew what happened, she was already twelve-years-old. She was growing up, and she was getting interested in learning how her mother did things around the house.

One Saturday morning in September, it was time to make sauerkraut. A big pile of mature cabbage heads lay on the kitchen floor. They had been picked out of their garden. Florence was busy stripping away the dirty, outer leaves of the cabbages. Meanwhile, Mom placed a head of cabbage into her shredder. It had a wooden frame, and she slid it up and down while applying pressure. Sharp knives sliced through the layered leaves.

It didn't take Mom very long to fill up a big pan with shredded cabbage. She dumped it into the bottom of a thirty-gallon crock. "Wash your feet, and wash them good if you want to help with the stomping," she instructed her kids. She then carefully added just the right amount of salt.

Florence was an eager volunteer. She had been running

around barefooted so her feet definitely needed a thorough cleaning. Once that was done, she climbed inside the big crock and began marching in place. "Why do we have to do this?" she asked.

"It gets the juice out," Mom replied as she continued operating her shredder. "The salty liquid has to cover up the cabbage so it doesn't spoil."

After a while, Florence got tired and bored, but she kept on stomping. When she heard a squishing sound, she looked down. "Juice is coming up between my toes!" she exclaimed.

"That's good," Mom replied. "You can get out of the crock. It's time to add another layer of cabbage and salt. Rose can do it next."

Mary Ann didn't get out of the tiresome task, either. She tromped around in the crock for a period of time, as well.

The older boys, George, Joe and Albert, were out in the field helping Dad. The younger boys, Ray, John, Ed and Francis, had disappeared, because they didn't want to have to do girls' work. Consequently, Florence's turn came around all too soon. She was about ready to climb back into the crock when Rose tattled, "Ah-ver! You didn't wash your feet again, and you went outside! I can see some dirt on your toes!"

As if a firecracker had just exploded, that got Mom's attention. "You've got to wash them every time you get back into the crock!" she scolded. "We're not just making kraut for the fun of it. It's a lot of work, and we've got to eat it."

The process of making sauerkraut took a long time. The girls could finally quit stomping when the juice level was above the shredded cabbage. When Dad came home, he carried the heavy crock, which was nearly full, down to the cellar. Florence watched as he put an old, rectangular shaped board inside the crock. It floated until he put a heavy rock on top of it. The weight would keep the cabbage submersed in the salty liquid.

Two weeks later, Mom said, "Florence, go down to the cellar and get a bowlful of sauerkraut. I'm going to make glace with it."

By the time, Florence got back into the kitchen, Mom was already mixing up her dumpling dough. She was also cooking some cubed potatoes in salted, boiling water.

When the potatoes were almost tender, she tore off little pieces of dough and dropped them into the boiling water. She then melted a little lard (rendered from a hog they'd home butchered) in a big frying pan and browned some chopped onions in it. To heat up the sauerkraut, she added it to the pan.

"The dumplings are starting to float," Florence announced.

"That means they're done," Mom informed her as she drained the boiling water into the sink. She added the dumplings and potatoes to the onions and sauerkraut and stirred everything together. "Call the others in for supper. It's time to eat."

Dad must have enjoyed the glace, because he took a second helping. "This is a good batch of sauerkraut," he complimented Mom.

"Never made any that ever spoiled," she replied proudly. "I've heard of people having to throw a whole batch away. It would be a shame to go to all that work and have it go wasted."

"Can you make spare ribs with sauerkraut and mashed potatoes for supper tomorrow night?" Florence asked.

"Sure," Mom replied. "That sounds good to me, too."

The next two years went quickly by for Florence. She was in eighth grade when Dad announced, "I bought a farm north of Iliff about 25 miles from here. We'll be moving in February."

"Will I be able to finish school at Padroni?" she asked.

"No," Dad replied. "There's a one-room schoolhouse not far from where we'll be living. It's called Hillview School. You kids will have to walk through the neighbor's pasture to get there."

The smaller school just had 24 students in eight grades. There was only one teacher, and she had her hands full trying to keep up with the different classes. "Florence, since you're one of the older students, could you help with the younger ones?"

"I'd like that," she replied enthusiastically. Florence thought back to how she'd struggled in first grade and realized how much progress she had made since then. It was a rewarding feeling helping the younger students.

In the meantime, Dad was talking with the other neighbors in the area about diversifying their farming operation to include a dairy. Many of them were selling Grade A milk to the Goodrich Dairy in Sterling. A truck came out their way daily to pick it up; therefore, it would just be one more stop for the driver.

One evening at supper, he informed the family, "Our neighbors have convinced me that we can make the most money by going into the dairy business. They tell me it's best to start out small with a herd of about 40 cows and build it up gradually."

"Our barn is only big enough for our workhorses. Are we going to get rid of them?" Florence asked.

"No, we'll still need them for field work. We'll raise feed for our livestock and have to build a lean-to onto the barn."

"Who's going to do that?" Mom asked. "We don't have money to hire anyone."

"George (oldest son) and I will," Dad answered. "We'll also have to build a milk house."

"Where are you going to build it?" Mom inquired.

"Right beside the windmill," Dad responded. "We'll put

a big cement tank inside the milk house and pump cool water into it. In the warmer months, we'll store our ten-gallon milk cans in it."

From what Dad had told the family, Florence could tell that starting up a dairy was going to alter their lives immensely. She enjoyed working outdoors so she was look-ing forward to the change.

After the buildings had been completed, Dad called everyone together who would be doing the hand milking. "Our milk will be tested," he stressed. "We don't want any of it to be rejected. Cleanliness is going to be very important."

Everyone knew what that meant. They were going to have to keep the barn and milk house spotless. Dad was very picky when it came to keeping things neat and clean. Florence knew that personality trait would make him an excellent Grade A dairy farmer. He proceeded to give fur-ther instructions, "When a cow enters the barn, you'll have to wash her bag with water and a rag. In the winter, you'll need to brush the snow off the cow's back with a curry-comb so it won't melt and get into the bucket."

"The barn will have to be swept out after each milking," Mom added, "and the gutter that runs along the one wall will need to be rinsed out really good."

As Florence listened, she thought that sounded like an awful lot of work to be done twice a day. But Dad contin-ued, "Whoever carries the pails of milk to the milk house has to pour it through a strainer into the ten-gallon cans. The cloth gauze filter needs to be thrown away after each milking."

"Where will we get more of them?" Florence asked.

"Don't worry about that," he replied. "I bought a big box of filters, because it's something we'll go through a lot of." He added, "We'll have to use hot, soapy water to wash out the strainer and buckets after each milking."

Mom, who quite often was the one with a sense of humor, laughed, "And we only have to milk our dairy cows 365 days out of the year. That is except for leap year, and then you'll have to do the chore an extra day."

Shortly after that, Dad bought a small herd of dairy cows. They were mostly Holsteins and a few Jersey crossbreeds. Before long, each of the cows had a name. Since the Lambrechts didn't have a pasture, their cows grazed over at the neighbor's place, which was just over two miles away. Florence and her siblings took turns riding their pony to herd them home for the evening milking. They had to drive their cows down the gravel road, because there wasn't another route by which they could get them home.

After being milked, the cows spent the night in the corral. When the next morning's milking was finished, someone saddled up the pony and herded the cattle back to the neighbor's pasture for a day of grazing.

A few of their cows were tame enough that they didn't need hobbles strapped onto their hind legs, but most of them had to wear the restraining device so they couldn't kick. The cows were always put in a stanchion, which would limit their movement. Since they were fed some ground-up corn, they were usually fairly content during the milking process.

Whenever Dad and the boys were working out in the fields, it was up to Mom and the three girls to handle the milking. Their cows produced an average of between 80 and 100 gallons of milk per day; therefore, it was quite a chore!

One summer evening, as the four of them were busily milking, Rose exclaimed out of nowhere, "Florence, I sure am glad you're such a fast milker! We get done a little faster because of you!"

Florence was seated on a t-shaped wood stool beside a big Holstein cow, and her hands were in rhythmic motion.

Milk was streaming into her pail. "I enjoy doing this a lot more than cleaning house."

"Not me," her older sister contradicted without thinking twice.

"I've timed myself," Florence replied. "I can milk a cow in six to seven minutes." She didn't know it at the moment, but milking cows by hand would be a chore she'd be doing for the next three decades of her life.

16
First American Generation of Gertners

O n May 23, 1925, Marcus (Mark) was born to John and Anna Gertner. On that same day, the New York Yankees defeated the Cleveland Indians 7-6 in a baseball game. The national pastime was a sport that Mark would thoroughly enjoy during his youth and adult years.

Like his three older brothers, he was born a first generation American, inheriting the rights of U. S. citizenship. Since his parents hadn't become naturalized citizens, they were still considered aliens from Russia by the government, but that didn't stop the couple from realizing the American dream. They worked hard in the early years for local, established farmers, and it finally paid off in 1928. A landlord gave them the opportunity to rent his land, and he provided a three-bedroom house for them to reside in. It was much larger and nicer than anything they'd ever lived in before. The small farm was located between Padroni and Iliff, Colorado. This is where the family weathered the Great Depression and the Dust Bowl years.

Just like at every other place they'd lived at since coming to America, they grew a garden. Of course, they always raised their cherished schwartzbeeren (blackberries). When the berries turned ripe in the fall of the year, Mark and his siblings were sent out to pick them. They had to walk through the yard, past their beet labor shack and cross a couple of barbed-wire fences to reach the garden. The bushes, which were loaded with clusters of fruit, were growing at the edge of a field.

The family also grew sugar beets, corn, hay and oats with only the help of workhorses. Early in his youth, Mark liked to watch how his father related to his favorite workhorse. All Dad had to do was call, "Jim, it's time to go to work!" Without fail, the giant reddish-brown horse would soon come to meet him with their other workhorses trailing behind.

"He definitely thinks you're his master," Mark observed. "Was he hard to train?"

"No, he catches on pretty quickly," Dad replied. "Horses like him don't come along very often. Most farmers need a team to pull a stacker, but Jim can handle it by himself. He follows my verbal commands to drop the hay in the front, middle or back part of the stack. It's like we're on the same page."

Since Jim was both smart and strong, he became a jack-of-all-trades around the farm. Workdays were long from six in the morning until six in the evening. When it was time to take an hour off for lunch, Mark helped Dad out by feeding the workhorses. He'd give each of them a gallon of oats. He got a kick out of watching Jim smack away on his favorite food. The giant workhorse was always ready to get back to work the second Dad called for him.

Mark would have enjoyed staying home year round and being his dad's right hand man, but he had to attend school. The bus that the Gertner children rode in had long benches along the sides and a double-sided bench down the center where students could sit and face either direction. Instead of side windows, it had canvas curtains. During the cold weather, they remained shut. On warmer days, the bus driver permitted the students to roll the curtains up, making the area wide open. Sometimes he allowed the boys to use their slingshots to shoot at pheasants as they traveled along the country roads picking up students.

One fall morning, as Mark and his older brother Ben boarded the school bus with their pockets full of rocks, the driver laughed before saying, "I can tell you boys are prepared to use your slingshots today. Go ahead and shoot them, but be careful."

Whenever the boys saw a pheasant, they aimed and fired. Time after time, their rocks simply landed on the ground until Ben finally got lucky. "I got one!" he shouted. The bus driver slammed on his brakes so that he could go after his game.

As Ben proudly boarded the bus, he handed the colorful bird to the driver, "You can have this, because I can't take it to school. Hope it tastes good."

"Well, thank you!" the bus driver responded in appreciation. "I'm sure it will. Excellent shot by the way."

In 1939, when Mark was fourteen-years-old, his parents paid a five dollar membership fee to the Rural Electrification Administration (R.E.A.) to obtain electric service to their farm. The first thing the construction crew did was stake out a path through their pasture. The teenager loved watching the men work before and after school. They dug holes by hand anywhere from three to four feet deep for the poles. After setting them, they strung the lines.

When the electricity was turned on, Mom didn't seem to know what to think about it. Dad tried his best to talk her into getting a new refrigerator and radio. She was used to doing everything the hard way, but she did finally admit, "These lights sure are bright. It's so much easier to see after dark."

"We really can afford a new refrigerator and radio," Dad persisted. "I don't want to go crazy and buy all kinds of new things like a lot of people are doing, but those two items would definitely be nice." She finally consented.

The family felt like they were becoming modern until they saw Mom ironing the old-fashioned way. She insisted that she didn't need an electric iron. She preferred using her sad iron, which had to be heated up on their coal stove. It was very hot, time-consuming work. Her cheeks grew rosy red as she worked her way through the stack of items needing pressed.

Mark was now in high school. His summer days were spent out in the field working alongside Dad and older brothers Johnnie, Dave and Ben. On many of those warm evenings, the boys still had plenty of energy to play softball. They didn't have any trouble recruiting their sisters Josie, Virginia, Esther and Anna Mary to participate in a game. Their playing field was in the cow pasture east of their barn. Mom and Dad and the younger siblings, Glen, Margie, Clara and Lawrence, gathered around and thoroughly enjoyed watching them demonstrate their athletic talents.

"Mark, you go ahead and pitch first tonight," Virginia suggested. "The last time we played, I had more pitching time than you did." They both enjoyed playing the same position.

The teenager with nearly black hair and blue eyes

warmed up by throwing a few pitches before the first batter stepped up to the plate. On some evenings, the strikes came consistently, and Dad would cheer, "Good pitch!" Other times, his pitches were wild, and snickers could be heard from the spectators. Since they were playing in the wide open spaces, batters could hit the ball a country mile.

While the game was competitive, it really didn't matter who won or lost. Their inexpensive pastime provided hours of fun for the entire family. Occasionally, the neighbors' sons came over to play with them. The extra players made an even better, more exciting game.

Softball wasn't the only thing that entertained Mark. He loved chasing his sisters and throwing "harmless" firecrackers at them. There weren't many places they could escape his pursuit, but Esther had an idea. "Hurry!" she yelled to her sisters. "Let's duck inside the outhouse. He won't be able to get us there."

It was cramped quarters for the girls, and it seemed eerily quiet outside. "Maybe he's given up chasing us," Esther whispered. About that time, a lit firecracker came through a tiny hole on the side of the outhouse. In a flash, the girls were out and running once again. Mark couldn't catch them now, because he was laughing so hard he could barely stand up.

His sisters weren't his only targets to receive an unexpected popping noise. One Saturday around the Fourth of July, Mark drove his mom and sister Josie into town for groceries. On the way home, they turned off the highway and onto their private gravel road. Almost immediately, they saw their landlord's dark green Chevy pickup parked on a hill beside the road. As they approached, they could tell that the older gentleman was being his usual nosy self. He was peering through a pair of binoculars. It was a perfect opportunity for the teenager to scare the tar out of him. He quickly lit a big firecracker; and as he drove by, he tossed it into the pickup's bed. Before long, they heard a loud bang. Mark got a good laugh out of his orneriness. Mom didn't see quite as much humor in the situation. She raised her voice and reprimanded him, "You should have never done that! We do have to stay on good terms with our landlord!"

Regardless, Mark wasn't worried about it. He had to force himself to quit chuckling so he could say, "I made a good shot and scored a point."

After graduation, Mark worked as a hired man for a neighbor. Since he was involved with farming, he received a deferment from serving in WW11. He and his brother Ben reached a mutual decision. They didn't feel right walking along the streets in town, seeing only a few young men left. Mark broke the news to the family, "Ben and I are going to enlist in the army."

Their parents respected their decision, but it was still hard on them. Johnnie, their oldest son, was already serving overseas. When the family waved goodbye to them, Dad expressed his fears, "They may never come home." Visible tears crept into his eyes. "We may never see them again." It took his children by surprise, because they rarely saw him overpowered by emotion.

The army sent the two brothers to Fort Lewis in Washington to be trained in electrical engineering basics. The purpose of the training was to teach them how to climb power poles so they could install communication lines. They were both stationed in the Philippines but at different bases.

Mark thought he was going to be a lineman. A lieutenant had different plans for him, though. He gave him the assignment of being the company clerk, because of his typing ability. Although it was an easy job, he didn't enjoy being around the generals. He also wasn't fond of the weather.

The country was extremely hot and sticky, and he longed for the climate of home. Playing baseball as a pastime was something that made army life more bearable for him.

The three Gertner brothers all made it through the war without any physical scars to remind them of it. When Mark returned home, his parents and siblings were grateful for his safe return. He met his new baby brother Don for the first time. Mom had given birth to him recently. The family was now complete with a total of 13 children.

After the excitement of Mark's return settled back down, he eagerly told his family of some famous men he'd met overseas, "Our companies got together and played baseball for recreation. Can you believe I played alongside Early Wynn and Joe Garagiola? They were both professional baseball players before they had to go overseas and serve in the war."

"That's really something," Dad commented.

"I thought I was a good ball player until I played with them!" Mark exclaimed. "I bunked right next to Hoyt Wilhelm. He was a minor league pitcher before going to the Philippines. Boy could he throw a good knuckleball. I'm guessing when he comes back to the states he'll make it as a professional." He laughed before adding, "We played in a field that sometimes had water buffaloes in it."

Ignoring the fact that her brother had met some great baseball players, Virginia piped up and exclaimed, "You should have been used to that! Sometimes we had to play around the cows in our pasture!"

17
The Blizzard of '49

When Mark Gertner and his brother Ben returned from WWII in 1945, they used the electrical training they had received from the army and became linemen. The construction company they worked for was erecting new substations, bringing in the "big voltage" to areas of Colorado, which were already served by small electric lines and generators. For several years, they worked within driving distance of their home. Later on, their jobs involved traveling to Nebraska, South Dakota and Wyoming. Their crew also brought electricity to desolate places where there was none at all.

Most of the time, the brothers worked with different lineman partners; but occasionally, they were paired up as a team. After one of those long work days, Mark looked at Ben completely satisfied with their accomplishment and declared, "It's almost unbeliev-able. In one day, we climbed and wired 150 R.E.A. poles. That's a new record."

"Yep," Ben replied grinning. "We couldn't of done it if the car wasn't waiting at the bottom of the pole to take us to the next one needing wired."

"Our jobs are dangerous and it's hard work, but we make top-notch wages," Mark summed up how he felt. He took off his cap to wipe away the sweat on his forehead.

Depending upon where they were working, the broth-ers came home for the weekend if possible. Mark's siblings always noticed if he plopped a sack of goodies on the buf-fet. Sometimes he shared the candy with them. Other times, they simply helped themselves, and he never got upset. He loved green apples. One weekend, he brought home a sack of them. His sister Virginia peeked inside the brown paper bag, hoping to find some sort of candy. "Green apples!" she exclaimed. "Yuk!"

"They're good," he answered before grinning. "The sourer—the better."

On the last weekend in December of 1948, Mark was invited to a neighbor's wedding dance. The Dutch Hop was being held upstairs above a store in the tiny town of Padroni. It didn't matter that there was a good turnout of young people for the occasion, because he only had his eye on Florence Lambrecht. They knew each other from school; but since she was four years younger, he hadn't paid much attention to her before. That evening was dif-ferent. They danced many polkas and waltzes together. As the Dutch Hop was about to end, he grew more nervous inside. He wanted to muster up the courage to ask her out on a date. Instead, he blurted out, "I had a good time."

"So did I," she replied, smiling radiantly.

As he drove home, he wondered, "How come I can climb

a 65-foot power pole and think nothing of it; but when it comes to asking Florence for a date, I chicken out?"

He would get another chance to ask her for their first date the following Sunday afternoon. As he was driving through the small town of Iliff, he noticed Florence and her sister Rose getting out of their car. He stopped and began the conversation with, "Can you believe how warm the weather is for the second day of January?"

"It's so nice you don't even need a coat," Florence commented, "but I bet we're in for a big change. It's way too warm for this time of the year."

"I think so, too," he replied. "Where are you headed?"

"We're going to a bridal shower," she responded.

"I was just on my way to the pool hall," he informed them. After a brief pause, he got brave enough to ask Florence for a date. She accepted, and he thought she seemed pleased. They agreed on the time; and as he drove away, he couldn't hold back a smile followed by a sigh of relief.

Mark spent the afternoon playing cards before going home to eat supper. He then quickly changed clothes. Since he was 23, he didn't tell his parents or siblings where he was venturing off to.

When he left home around six o'clock in the evening, it wasn't snowing at all. Still, there wasn't a doubt in his mind that the weather was going to be taking a major turn for the worse. He knew it might be foolish, but he decided to risk it. He had a date he definitely wanted to keep.

Florence lived with her parents, seven miles north and six miles east of his parents' farm. Just before he turned east onto a gravel road, huge snowflakes began hitting the windshield of his brown 1935 Chevy four-door car. The wind had picked up considerably, and the intensity of the storm was rapidly turning into a blizzard. He went over a bridge and tried going up a shallow grade, but it was too slick. His car stalled, and it took a moment for him to realize that he was stuck out in the middle of nowhere. More than likely, another vehicle wouldn't be coming down the road. If only he had thought ahead, he'd be safe at home.

Fortunately, he was familiar with the territory. He knew exactly where he was stranded, but no one else knew his whereabouts. "It might be possible to walk to the nearest farmhouse," he reasoned. It was dark out, so he left his lights on just in case he'd have to seek shelter in his car. He had only gone about 100 feet when he was forced to hurry back to his vehicle and ride out the blizzard with a light jacket, a heavy army coat, no gloves and the large box of chocolates meant for Florence.

Sixty hours later, on Wednesday morning, Mark could tell that the blizzard had finally blown itself out. The wind had switched directions and was coming out of the south-west. He was thankful that the driver's door wasn't blocked shut. A drift, as high as his car, had formed several feet away. There was no way he was going to drive out of his predicament like he planned on doing all along.

It was 3½ miles to Florence's house. He used fence posts as a guide to walk over the wavy ocean of huge, white snowdrifts. The harsh conditions soon took their toil on him. He was exhausted and extremely cold.

As he approached their farmyard, he could tell that the Lambrechts were just finishing up with the morning milking. Florence's dad and several of her brothers were carrying buckets to their milk house. When her father spotted him, he shouted, "What on earth of you doing here?"

"My car is stranded by the bridge that goes over the Lewis Canyon Creek," he replied, quickly giving him a visual picture of its location. "That's where I rode out the blizzard since Sunday evening. I was on my way over here to pick up Florence for a date."

Mark was hurried into their living room to get warmed up. It seemed dark in their house, because his eyes were used to the bright snow. After his eyesight adjusted to his surroundings, he realized a curious family had gathered around to find out what was going on. He felt self-conscious, being the center of attention.

"We heard on the radio that this was the worst blizzard of the century," Florence spoke shyly. "Lots of people were stranded in their vehicles, but I never thought you'd try to keep our date. I assumed you were safe at home."

"My parents don't know where I am," he replied in a concerned tone. "I'd ask to borrow your phone so I could call them to put their minds at ease, but they don't have one."

"They're probably worried sick about you," Florence's father commented. "You won't be going anywhere until the road grader comes through, which might be several days from now. None of our tractors could pull you out."

"Are you finished with the chores?" Florence's mother asked.

"We should be done in about ten minutes," her father replied.

"Mark must be starved. I'll start cooking breakfast," she said before bustling into the kitchen.

Strangely enough, he wasn't hungry as a bear. Normally, Mark would have gladly gone outdoors to help the men finish the chores, but not today. "How do you feel?" Florence interrupted his thoughts.

"Not too bad considering what I've been through," he replied. He paused before telling her about his ordeal. "The hardest part was sitting on my feet. Then my legs went to sleep. I'd have to stretch my legs and sit on my feet again to keep them from freezing. Other than that, the cold never bothered me much."

"I don't know how you stood it!" Florence exclaimed. "Most people would have frozen to death."

"I'm used to it," he replied. "Us linemen work out in cold weather all day long. When I come home for weekends, my brothers Dave, Ben, Glen and I sleep in the beet labor shack. In the wintertime, we sleep with our shoes on, because it's not heated or insulated very well. I wouldn't be surprised if lots of snow blew into the shack during this blizzard."

"I didn't know you slept over there," Florence sympathized with him.

"I don't mind," he answered. "We just have a three-bedroom house. With 13 of us kids, it's way too crowded. When the weather gets really bad, we do sleep in the house on the living room floor."

"It's probably good you were used to cold temperatures," she concluded. "Otherwise, you might not be here."

"The thought never entered my mind that I wasn't going to make it out okay," he informed her. "I didn't dare fall asleep. I knew that would be the worst thing I could do." He chuckled before saying, "By the way, I ate the box of chocolates I bought for you. They didn't taste too good come the second day."

"That's okay," she replied.

When it was time for breakfast, everyone gathered around the kitchen table. Mark felt bad, because he only ate a little. It certainly wasn't because of Florence's mother's cooking.

Over the next couple of days, his appetite came back slowly, and he caught up on his sleep. Health wise he felt fine, but he was getting restless. On Friday, the snow plow finally opened the roads and dug out his car. He thanked the Lambrechts for their hospitality and headed for home.

Come to find out, his family hadn't been worried about him at all. They thought he'd gone down to Iliff to play pool or cards. They assumed he had stayed with his uncle and aunt who lived in town to ride out the powerful blizzard.

Shortly after Mark's blizzard experience, he took Florence to a Dutch Hop. They danced a few times before he told her, "My feet are tingling. They just don't feel right."

"Maybe you should go to the doctor," she suggested, knowing he didn't like going there.

The next day, he reluctantly went to the doctor and found out that he had frostbitten feet. The doctor went on to explain that they would probably give him plenty of trouble for quite a while. His diagnosis proved to be right. Mark's feet began bothering him so much that he didn't want to walk on them. His family stared at him as he crawled around the house. He certainly couldn't go to work. How could he climb power poles with painful feet?

To the family's amazement, however, he managed to get back to courting fairly soon. "Can you haul me out to my car in your wagon?" he asked his ten-year-old brother.

"Okay," Lawrence agreed.

It had rained recently. Mark felt rather silly, sitting in a little red wagon while his younger brother was struggling to pull his heavy load through the mud. It was no use—they were stuck. "Go get Margie or Clara to push," he suggested.

Both of them came outdoors to help. The three of them were able to get the wagon rolling once again. After getting into his car, Mark told the three of them to take whatever

Mark Gertner and Florence Lambrecht's
Wedding Day, January 31, 1950.
The bride's parents' Pete and Magdalena are to her left, and the groom's parents' Anna and John are to his right.

they wanted out of his stash of candy. That was his way of showing appreciation.

At the end of August, Mark and Florence got engaged. In keeping with their German-Russian tradition, they definitely planned on getting married in the winter when farm work was at its slowest pace. They set a wedding date of January 24, 1950, only to find out that his sister Josie had already chosen that day. So they changed their wedding plans for the following Tuesday.

Mark asked his brothers Ben and Glen and sisters Virginia and Esther to stand up for him. Florence's brothers Albert and Joe and sisters Rose and Mary Ann were the ones she chose to be in their wedding party. The couple walked down the aisle on January 31, 1950, to recite their

Dutch Hop band provided polka and waltz music at Mark and Florence's wedding, playing an accordion, trumpet, dulcimer and trombone. Wedding dances were a tradition that German-Russian immigrants brought with them from the Old Country.

vows at St. Anthony's Catholic Church. It was the same church where both of their parents had been married.

After the ceremony, they invited their guests to a meal at the Schell Chateau, which was followed by a Dutch Hop. Florence's Uncle Alex had a four-member polka band. He played the trumpet while the other members played an accordion, trombone and dulcimer.

Just before the music started, Florence pinned a fancy handkerchief on her wedding gown. It was a long-standing practice for a man to pin money on it before dancing with her. After each song ended, she removed the money. She didn't get much rest time in between dances.

Unlike the previous generation, Mark and Florence's Dutch Hop ended at midnight. It didn't start up at six

Members of Florence and Mark Gertner's wedding party are dancing a polka. In foreground: *Virginia Gertner (groom's sister) and Albert Lambrecht (bride's brother.)* In background: *Esther Gertner (groom's sister) and Joe Lambrecht (bride's brother.)*

o'clock the following morning and last for two days like their parents had. Little by little, old-fashioned German-Russian customs were changing, while others remained steadfast.

18
Mark and Florence
Suz's parents

As newlyweds, the young Gertner couple made a risky decision. Mark quit his career as a lineman, because he didn't want to travel and be away from home. It wasn't the kind of life he envisioned with a new wife and the family they would surely have. They thought it would be fairly easy for him to find another job, but it wasn't. He soon grew tired of being unemployed.

One Saturday, they decided to attend an auction for something to do. They ran into Florence's Uncle Clarence, and Mark told him that he was interested in farming. "I know of a small farm by Cedar Creek that would be ideal for you. Mrs. Johnson is looking for a good renter," he mentioned. "I farmed for her years ago and would be happy to put in a good word for you."

With Uncle Clarence's helpfulness, the deal was sealed. On March 1, 1950, just a month after their marriage, the newlyweds moved from the apartment they were living in to the rented farm. A promising future lay ahead for them.

The first thing they needed to do was furnish their small house. For Florence, it only seemed natural to attend auctions and search for bargains. While she was growing up, her parents (Pete and Magdalena) had routinely attended the public sales on Saturday afternoons. Her mom and dad liked to buy things that went cheap and were in good condition for their dairy farm and home. So it wasn't surprising that they ran into them at the next auction. They had plenty of time to visit with one another between items they were interested in.

Mark and Florence were definitely going to bid on a good-looking coal stove. Since it was one of the nicest things up for sale that day, it would be sold near the end of the auction. After standing for hours, Mom told Florence, "Your father always outlasts me. Whenever I get tired, I go to the car and wait for him. I think I'm going to call it a day. Hope you get what you want."

About half-an-hour later, the auctioneer drew the crowd's attention to the coal stove. After some brisk bidding, the couple was thrilled that they got the bid. "I can cook and bake with the stove during the winter, and it'll also heat up the kitchen," Florence expressed her plans for it. "Hopefully, the diesel stove that we have in our living room will keep the rest of the house warm enough."

Auctions weren't the only place that the newlyweds bought items to furnish their rented home. They purchased a used wringer washing machine and a three-burner kerosene stove from Mark's Uncle's neighbor. Florence planned on cooking and baking with the kerosene stove during the warmer months.

Once their household was set up, the pair began concentrating on what they needed to begin farming with. "It was generous of your parents to loan us a team of workhorses for a year and give us enough hay and grain to feed them," Florence said.

"That it was," Mark agreed. "The way I see it, we still need to buy another team of workhorses, a few cattle, chickens, pigs, a used tractor and as many farming implements as we can afford." And that is exactly what they did.

Before long, Mark was working out in the field planting hay, barley, corn and sugar beets. Like both sets of their parents had learned years before, raising beets involved a lot of manual labor. His brother Dave and sister-in-law Rose were looking for work. They hired them to help with the thinning, hoeing and harvesting of the crop.

Harvest began the first part of October. Not much had changed since the old days. A team of workhorses was used to pull their horse-drawn beet puller. It only loosened the soil around the large roots, one row at a time. Every single beet still needed to be manually pulled out of the ground, topped with a beet knife, loaded onto a truck with a beet fork and hauled to the dump.

As soon as their sugar beets were all dug, corn harvest got underway. Just like in the days of his youth, Mark picked it by hand. The only difference being – he no longer was working alongside his father and three older brothers. He had to handle the big job alone. A team of workhorses pulled the hayrack up and down the field on his commands. He grabbed an ear of dried corn with the hook of his husking tool and pitched it over the low-boarded sides into the hayrack. It took him two weeks to get the last major field work done before winter set in.

Six years later, Mark, Florence and their three kids went to visit his parents (John and Anna) who lived about seven miles from them. "We've been on this place for 28 years, and your mom and I have decided that this is going to be our last crop," Dad spoke with mixed emotions. "It's time we retire and move into town."

Mark was taken by surprise. "Aren't you too young for that?" Then, for the first time in a long while, he took a good look at both of them. To him, they'd suddenly aged.

"Not as young as we used to be," Dad replied matter-of-factly. "Time marches on. When I told the landlord that we were quitting, he immediately mentioned that he wanted you to take over renting this farm."

Mark already knew what his opinion was, but he glanced over at Florence, "We'll talk it over first, and let you know what we decide."

"Sounds good," Dad answered. "We're planning on having our farm sale early next winter. We've already been looking for a house to buy in Sterling. We want something that is within walking distance of church. It doesn't have to be anything fancy."

They visited for a while longer before Mark stood up and said, "We best head back to the poor farm. It's about milking time."

During the short drive home, he asked Florence, "What d'ya think about moving?"

"I'm for it," she answered without hesitation. "The farm where we're at now has been a good starting point, but it's just too small to support us. We'll soon be having our fourth child."

"I agree," he responded enthusiastically. "I'll let my parents know tomorrow. After I do that, I'll make a trip into Sterling to tell the landlord."

The next day it was made official. Mark and Florence were going to be moving to his boyhood farm.

The fall went quickly by. On Thanksgiving Day, Mark, Florence and family went over to his parents' home to celebrate the holiday. After eating a big meal, they sat around and visited. Mom told them, "On the 11th of December, I've got to take my test to become a citizen." By the tone of her voice, it was obvious that she was nervous about it.

"She's worried that she won't pass," Dad explained. "She didn't want to become a citizen 15 years ago when I did. I like being able to vote and have a strong opinion about the government." Everyone snickered at the last remark. They all knew it was true. Political discussions were a favorite subject of his.

"I just don't like courtrooms. They remind me of when we first came to Ellis Island. We never passed inspection, and we had to go before a Special Inquiry Board in a room that looked like a courtroom," Mom clarified the reason for her fear. "I was so scared. A bad experience like that sticks with you."

"My parents just became citizens this past June," Florence chimed in.

"The test is supposed to be about United States history and the government. Did they think it was hard?" Mom asked.

"They never said anything, so I assume it wasn't."

The next time Mark and Florence saw his parents, Mom eagerly told them, "It took me 45 years to become a U. S. citizen, but I'm one now."

Even after all the years that his mom had been in the United States, Mark could still see signs of her German-Russian roots. She always wore her long hair up in a bun.

Whenever she went outdoors in chilly weather, a scarf habitually covered her head.

As the winter of 1957 was showing signs of spring, Mark and Florence moved from one farm to the other one. For Mark especially, it seemed strange to be living in the same house on the same land that his parents had for so many years. They had been good stewards of the land. As the second generation to live there, they wanted to do their best to maintain and hopefully improve what had been previously established.

On a beautiful May afternoon, Mark was walking at the edge of the field beside their beet labor shack, and he came upon his parents' blackberry garden. They had planted it years ago when they first moved to the small farm. There wasn't a year that went by, that it didn't produce delicious fruit. Upon closer examination, he noticed tiny, two leaf plants were sprouting up everywhere. Work could wait; he had to tell his wife about his discovery. He rushed into the house with excitement showing on his face. "Guess what I just found!"

"I don't have a clue," she responded. Her brown eyes expressed curiosity.

"Lots of blackberries are coming up in Mom and Dad's garden. I never even thought about inheriting it, but we did. Now, all we have to do is care for it, and we'll have berries for years to come."

19
The
Blackberry Garden

By 1969, Mark and Florence Gertner's family was complete. They still lived at the small farm where he grew up. It was a wonderful place to raise their ten children: Delores, Suz, Tom, Patty, Judy, Luke, Mary, Jackie, Joann and Dan. The farm had become a family operation for them. Everyone who was old enough to help out with the chores and field work did so.

Their kitchen table was a gathering place for the big family three times a day. The kids knew which chairs Dad and Mom's were, but the rest of the seats were filled on a first come basis. With the dozen of them crowded around the table, not much elbow room was available. A lot of the foods that Mom prepared had roots to their farm. They had their own beef, pork, chicken, eggs, milk, cream, roasti-neers (corn on the cob), sunflower seeds, plus a variety of vegetables and fruits. Their two gardens were strategically located in different parts of the farm, because they got more than their fair share of hail. Sometimes one garden didn't get as much damage as the other one did.

Even though a few other things such as tomatoes and cucumbers were planted in their one garden, the family always referred to it as their blackberry garden. It got its name, because that is what was primarily grown there.

On a sunny May afternoon, Mom drove their pickup while sixteen-year-old Suz and her siblings rode along. It was a short drive to their blackberry garden. Years of following the same path had created a dirt road, which ran alongside their pasture.

While the younger kids were hoeing out weeds by the cucumbers and tomatoes, Mom and her older children were going to thin out the extra blackberries, which had come up voluntarily. Suz, who was a rookie at the job, asked, "How far apart should we space them?"

"About a foot," her mother replied. "That way they'll have room to bush out. It will also leave enough space between the plants, so we can get in there and pick the berries when they're ripe."

The teenager looked down at the greenery that was interwoven together. "I'm confused!" she exclaimed. "It's hard to tell the young blackberry plants from the weeds."

"A little bit," Mom agreed, "but they do look different." She singled out a plant and hoed around it. "See here's one." She paused for a moment and added, "Lots of them came up this year."

"I remember when the blackberry patch used to be at the edge of the field next to our beet labor shack," Suz recalled. "Why did we move it?"

"Dad wanted to plant hay in that field," she explained. "You don't have to irrigate hay very often, so the berries probably wouldn't have gotten enough water unless it rained a lot. Plus, the soil wears out after a while when you grow the same thing in it year after year. Your grandparents had them there for years."

After they worked for a while, the area was dotted with blackberry plants that were around four inches tall. At least for a while, the weeds weren't a problem. They'd probably have to come back later and hoe out the new ones that popped up. The garden would be flood irrigated every time Dad irrigated the row crop that was growing right beside it.

Typically, the fruit was ready to be picked right around the beginning of school. This fall was no exception. Most afternoons after getting home from school, Suz, her brothers and sisters would walk over to the garden to pick them. The smooth skinned blackberries grew in clusters of about five to seven. Invariably, the whole group couldn't be plucked clean in one motion. One or several of them were still too green to be eaten; consequently, the ripe ones had to be "cherry picked." They selected deep purple berries or those with dull black skins. They were the ripest, sweetest ones. Mom made pies, strudels, dumplings or jelly with them. If she didn't have an immediate use for the blackberries, she froze them.

On Saturday afternoon, Mom made an extra request, "This afternoon you need to go pick some blackberries for Grandma and Grandpa Gertner. I know they really appreciate getting them."

Once again, the berry pickers headed over to the garden as a group. It had become very familiar territory lately. They were beginning to feel like they lived out in the garden.

The next morning after Suz and her family attended church, they stopped over at her grandparents' house for a visit. Like usual, Grandma was wearing an apron over her dress. When Mom handed her the bowlful of blackberries, a beautiful smile lit up her face. "Thank you so much," she said gratefully before carrying the fruit into the kitchen. It was easy to tell that Grandma was already cooking their dinner, because an enticing aroma drifted from the kitchen into the living room.

"Those will taste mighty good," Grandpa spoke up. He was sitting in his favorite chair in the corner of the living room. "We have a little garden here in town, but it doesn't turn out very good. It was a lot easier to raise gardens on the farm."

By her grandparents' reaction, Suz could tell Mom was right. They truly did appreciate the produce from their garden.

Soon Grandma came back into the living room. She had emptied and washed the bowl. She handed it back to Mom.

Now it was Grandpa's turn to go into the kitchen. Suz already knew what that meant, for a tradition had been established. He emerged carrying enough ice cream bars for each of his grandkids. On other Sundays, he might hand out candy. After visiting a while longer, it was time to head back to the farm.

At that particular time in Suz's life, she didn't fully understand how much blackberries meant to her ancestors. Ever since she could remember, they were just a normal part of her family's diet. She'd grown up with blackberries and loved picking them right off the bush and plopping a few into her mouth. They tasted wonderful, and she couldn't resist going, "Mmm."

The grocery store certainly never sold any fruits that tasted remotely like them. Suz didn't realize blackberries were exclusive to the German-Russian culture until her high school teacher organized an International Supper. Mrs. Stasenka's home economics students and their moms were invited to the event. Each student was requested to bring a covered dish from her heritage. Since she didn't know how to cook any German-Russian dishes, Mom had to come to the rescue, but she was indecisive. "Do you want to take homemade wurst (German sausage) or blackberry strudel?"

"Make whichever one you want to," Suz replied. "They're both good."

On the spring evening of the International Supper, they arrived at the high school gym to find tables lined with foods from different cultures. Mom placed her dish of blackberry strudel on the table by the other desserts. She had made it from frozen berries that they had picked last fall.

When it was time to eat, everyone got to choose from Italian, Mexican, Lebanese and quite a few German-Russian dishes. A smorgasbord of flavors filled their plates.

On the way home, Mom remarked, "Mrs. Stasenka put a lot of effort into organizing the International Supper. I really enjoyed it. I hope she does it again next year."

"She will," Suz answered confidently. "She's got lots of energy. It was a neat experience to taste foods from different cultures. We always take ours for granted. We don't think it's special, but it is. Maybe that's what Mrs. Stasenka wanted her students to learn tonight."

20
Riverside Cemetery

O n Thursday, April 30, 1970, Suz was a senior in high school. Just before noon, she went to English class. Mrs. Parker, their teacher, was beaming when she began speaking, "Class, I have some exciting news to share today. Last fall, Suz submitted a poem titled, "Dreamworld" to the National High School Poetry Press. Her poem has been selected to appear in their upcoming publication, "Young America Sings." The anthology will include poems, which were chosen from high schools in the western United States."

The announcement surprised Suz probably more than it did any of her classmates. At that particular moment, she really did feel like she was in a dreamworld, floating on a cloud without a care in the world. "My poem is actually going to be printed in a book!" she marveled. "It doesn't seem possible."

"You can have the letter announcing your accomplishment," Mrs. Parker said as she handed it to her stunned student. "Congratulations and keep on writing."

That afternoon, Suz was in home economics class. She couldn't put her finger on it, but she had an eerie feeling something terrible was wrong. It wasn't that she was having a bad day, because so far everything was going great. For some unknown reason, she felt anxious.

The instant Suz got home from school, she was planning on telling her mother the exciting news. The house was unusually quiet. She found Mom lying on her bed, reading a prayer book. She immediately knew something was wrong. "Ed (Mom's brother) called a little while ago and told me that Grandma Lambrecht had a very bad stroke this afternoon. The doctor doesn't think she is going to make it. After we do the milking and eat supper, I'm going to go to the hospital."

At five o'clock, Mom went to help with the chores like usual. She was busy milking a cow by hand when Judy came rushing out to the barn. "Aunt Geraldine called. She wanted me to tell you that Grandma passed away."

After we ate supper, the family made a trip into town to Grandpa's house where the rest of the families were gathering. Suz didn't quite know how to absorb all the sadness that filled the air. Up until now, death had been a stranger to her. It always happened to someone else's family. This was different, though. It didn't seem possible that her first grandparent was really gone. She died just one day before her 71st birthday. Why only last Sunday, she'd sat a couple of pews behind Grandma Lambrecht in church. Even at her age, she was a natural brunette. She was wearing a pretty hat, fancy earrings and a necklace. She'd looked radiantly happy.

On Saturday, Magdalena Hochnadel Lambrecht's family and friends gathered at St. Anthony's Catholic Church to honor her life on earth and say goodbye. After Mass, the hearse slowly led a procession across town to Riverside Cemetery. Her parents were also buried there—far from the roots of their birthplace of Schuck, Russia.

On Wednesday, February 20, 1974, Suz was at her job working when Mom called and relayed in a composed voice, "Grandpa Lambrecht passed away a little while ago." The family had known for a while that this day was coming, so the news wasn't unexpected. Still, the reality of death hurt beyond words.

John Peter (Pete) Lambrecht had been battling cancer. He was 78. Both of Mom's parents were gone now.

When the family was gathered at the funeral home, a nun, who was serving the parish, stepped to the front of the room. She wanted to express her condolences to the family. She also went on to say, "One of the last times I visited with Pete, he'd reached the stage where he wasn't able to keep food down. He told me the saddest part of all was that he could no longer receive Holy Communion."

By his comment, it was obvious to Suz what was of utmost importance to Grandpa in his dying days. While his body failed him, his faith had remained steadfast.

A Mass of Christian Burial was held at St. Anthony's Catholic Church on Saturday. As mourners left the church, a blustery north wind whipped at their faces like the sting of death. At Riverside Cemetery, they huddled under a green tent, trying to keep warm. The edges of it were flapping in the wind. Pete was buried beside his second wife Magdalena Hochnadel Lambrecht—far from the village of Pfeifer, Russia, where he was born. His parents were buried on American soil just a short distance away.

Death had not been a stranger to Pete during his lifetime. He'd lost his first wife and baby during childbirth. He found love again and remarried in 1921. In 1952, their daughter Mary Ann was swiftly taken away as the result of a car accident. Suz recalled him saying, "There's nothing harder than losing a child." Her grave was only a few feet from theirs.

On Sunday morning, May 15, 1988, Suz, her husband Ben and their three kids were at home when her parents stopped by after attending church. They told them that Grandpa Gertner had been taken by ambulance to the hospital earlier that morning.

In the afternoon, Suz went over to Mom and Dad's house to find out how he was doing. "I don't think he'll be here come morning," Dad replied simply.

John Gertner, Sr., who often said he'd been blessed with a good, long life, died peacefully at six o'clock that evening. He was 91. Suz lovingly recalled Grandpa saying, "The old have to die to make way for the young." Fittingly, that is exactly what happened. His granddaughter Patty gave birth to her first child earlier that day. Her baby daughter was born in the same hospital where he'd spent his final hours as a patient.

Wednesday morning, the funeral was held at St. Anthony's Catholic Church. A light mist was falling as the procession made its way to Riverside Cemetery. For some, the gentle spring rain may have seemed like an inconvenience; but if John had been there, he would have welcomed the rain. The crops needed the moisture, and he was a farmer at heart. He'd learned how to farm from his father in faraway Volmer, Russia.

At the age of 21, he'd saw the Spanish Flu sweep across the country at a pandemic level. It had swiftly claimed the life of his mother. Like his parents, he was being buried at Riverside Cemetery, which was near the shallow South Platte River. The winding river soaked up the misting rain and further downstream some farmer would use it to irrigate his crops.

Since Anna Ertle Gertner lived to be 101, Suz had reached the stage where she appreciated what her last living grandparent had to offer. She got to know her on a more personal, one-on-one basis after Grandpa passed away. They had been married for 68 years, and she was lonely.

During the morning of Thursday, January 30, 2003, Anna departed from her earthly journey. Throughout her century of living, she'd seen many younger loved ones being called, "Home." She probably wondered, "Why not me?" One of her favorite sayings was, "You've got to take it as it comes." That held true in another statement Suz heard her say, "I'll stay here until the Lord is ready for me."

By the time that happened, nearly everything Anna enjoyed in life had been stripped away except her faith. On one visit, Grandma Gertner told Suz, "I can't even remember all of my children's names anymore." A sadness filled her voice and her eyes. Although she had 13 names to remember, few children had a more caring mother.

On Tuesday morning, several generations gathered at St. Anthony's Catholic Church to celebrate her long life. At the end of the service, the priest announced, "I know it's cold out; but for all those who are able, let's go lay Anna to rest." Suz felt honored to be a part of that.

Anna would not have chosen any other plot than beside her husband John and in the same cemetery where her parents were buried. As a young girl, she'd experienced life in the village of Volmer, Russia, far from the America that finally accepted her. She'd known the pain of being called a, "Dirty Roosian." At the time of her death, Anna's ancestry included: 13 children, 65 grandchildren, seven step-grandchildren, 116 great grandchildren and four great, great grandchildren. She helped pave an easier life for them and those still to follow.

About a year later, Suz and her husband Ben set off on a sentimental journey. They went to Riverside Cemetery with the intention of taking photos of the headstones of each of her great grandparents and grandparents. Since they weren't sure where most of them were buried, they had to do a lot of searching.

While scanning the rows of gravestones, they accidentally stumbled upon the tombstone her parents had bought. She had no idea they had already purchased a plot there. Reality suddenly hit her; they were the next generation in line to be called "home" by the roll call up yonder.

When they found the last marker they were looking for, Suz got sentimental. Remarkably, her entire family tree—dating as far back as her great grandparents—was resting under the magnificent trees of Riverside Cemetery. For that reason alone, it held a special place in her heart. She also felt very grateful that all of her ancestors put their trust in God's promise of everlasting life. They'd nurtured the seed of faith and passed it down to their descendants.

The photos Ben took of the tombstones turned out clear

as a bell. The names and dates of their births and deaths were solidly set in stone. They were the skeleton facts of her ancestors. Suz wished she could have heard firsthand the everyday stories of those buried there. For that, it was too late. Sadly, those stories were locked away from present and future generations.

21
Fields of Life

Back in the summer of 1981, Suz, her husband Ben and kids were visiting her parents at the farm. The conversation took an unexpected turn when Dad announced, "This will be our last year of farming. I told the landlord that we'll be moving into town by the end of January."

Suz was very surprised. Dad seemed entirely too young to be quitting something he loved, but she never questioned his decision. She had a hard time picturing her parents living in town. They'd been farming since before she was born, and it was their way of life.

Come September, the new renter asked if he could begin working the ground where the crops had already been harvested. "That'll be okay," Dad replied, "but I don't want you to plow under the blackberry garden, yet. We're still picking them. I'll let you know when we're through."

The farmer just smiled. He realized that blackberries must be something special to the Gertner family. "Where's the garden located?"

"It's on the south corner of the 25-acre field that's on the east side of our property," Dad replied.

Like every other fall, the family picked brimming bowlfuls of ripe berries. They'd carried on the tradition that Grandpa and Grandma had started just over half a century ago on the small farm.

In the past, Mom didn't have to worry about saving much blackberry seed. Nature took care of the reseeding for her. This year, she collected seeds for the new garden they would be planting in town. Each time she rinsed off a bowlful of berries, lots of tiny seeds got into her water. She carefully poured the rinse water through a piece of old cloth, trapping them on the material. She tied the little bundle shut with a handmade cloth tie and hung the pouch out on the clothesline to dry.

After their farm auction in January, Mom and Dad packed up their things. Once again, blackberry seeds were making a move. This time they were only going 15 miles, nothing like the major journey the original seeds from Russia had made when they traveled to America.

In the spring, Dad and Mom tossed the fine seeds in the area where they wanted blackberries to grow. They also planted a variety of vegetables in the other portion of their small garden.

The blackberries came up like clockwork. All summer long, the bushes grew like a weed, flowered and got green clusters of berries on them. Everything was looking great for a delicious blackberry pie until the birds discovered that they were nearly ripe enough to pick. Once they got a taste of the fruit, they decided to peck away on more than their fair share.

After a couple of years of putting up with the birds, Mom decided it wasn't worth trying to grow blackberries in town. She eliminated them from the garden; but before doing so, she wisely kept seed just in case someone would want them in the future. She had learned from her parents (Pete and Magdalena) to save things that might come in handy down the road. As a young girl, the depression years had made a lasting impression upon her.

A few years later, their son Tom moved to the country, and he asked Mom if she had anymore blackberry seed. She knew exactly where the homemade pouches were stored. She gladly handed him one.

Tom grew a large garden. By fall, he had a bumper crop of blackberries. He invited his parents and siblings over to pick as many as they wanted.

Once again, Mom saved seed after washing off the berries. It seemed like such a waste just to wash them down the drain. Her thinking was, "You never know who might want some of them." She squirreled them away where they'd be safe…but not forgotten.

It was a good thing she did. Suz, Ben and family had moved from Colorado to Kansas. On one of their visits, Ben mentioned, "I think it would be fun to grow strawberries."

"I raised them for a while," Mom replied. "We got a few strawberries, but the worms ate most of them."

"You know what else I think would be fun to grow!" Ben exclaimed enthusiastically, "blackberries!"

"Those do sound good," Suz jumped in the conversation. "It's been years since I've eaten them."

"I've got some seed if you want it," Mom offered.

"We'll take some," Ben replied.

"I don't think you'll like blackberries," Suz cautioned. "You didn't grow up eating them, and they do have a taste all their own."

"It's fun to grow new things," he replied. "Besides they're part of your heritage."

On the trip back to Kansas, a bulging pouch of seeds was packed away in one of their suitcases. When they got home, Suz stored them in a cupboard next to other packets of seeds she'd bought at the store. She had every intention of planting them come spring, but life got too busy.

In fact, several springs passed before the couple remembered the blackberry seed. It finally dawned on them that the tiny seeds Mom had given them were descendants of the original ones brought clear from Russia. Plus, a century of time had passed, and a tiny piece of her ancestors' legacy was still remarkably intact. They were an heirloom.

Since Suz couldn't remember what blackberries looked like when they came up, she thought it best to plant some in an old flower pot. She sat it next to the window to give it sunshine. Their intention was to transplant them outdoors when they got big enough.

Within a week, two-leafed plants were dotting the soil's surface. For a while, they grew like a weed, but she was concerned with how fragile their stems looked. She didn't remember them being so spindly when they raised them on the farm. Soon, one after another began drooping and withering away.

The five remaining plants were growing any which way but straight. It was obvious that they were straining to reach enough sunlight. "Do you think we should transplant them outside?" Ben asked.

"I don't think they're strong enough to make it," Suz replied. So they continued to baby them indoors. As weeks went by, she could tell they weren't growing nearly fast enough to produce berries by fall. The time had come to relocate them regardless of the consequences.

On the steaming hot morning of July 1st, they carefully transplanted their struggling plants at the edge of their garden. They knew the heat would take its toll on them. Almost instantly, the leaves began wilting.

By the following morning, all but one of the plants had dried up. The last survivor didn't look the best, but it was hanging in there. Suz and Ben knew if this one didn't make it, they wouldn't have blackberries until next year for sure. They did their best to take very good care of it.

In a few weeks, the surviving blackberry began to flourish. By this time, they didn't just think of it as a plant. It had become the couple's goal to successfully start blackberries in a new territory like Suz's great grandparents had done a century ago. None of her aunts and uncles still grew blackberries; it was up to the grandchildren (her generation) to carry it on. If they let the family tradition of growing blackberries die out, it couldn't be recaptured. Not a store in the country carried any of that particular seed.

One morning, as Suz watered the blackberry, she admired how tall the bush had grown. Its leaves were a lovely, healthy green color. All of a sudden it dawned on her, "We should name our plant Ancestry. That would be a fitting name for her. After all, she's an offspring of the seed my great grandparents brought over from Russia, which makes her very special. We've invested so much time and effort into her that she's no longer just stems, leaves, flowers and clusters of tiny green berries. She's part of our family - certainly part of our heritage."

That evening Suz told Ben, "I think we should call our blackberry Ancestry." She was hoping he didn't think she'd lost her marbles.

His eyes lit up, and he smiled before saying, "I like that name. It fits." He then changed the subject slightly. "I can build a cage around Ancestry and cover it with plastic. That'll block the hot Kansas wind from getting to her."

The couple agreed that would be a smart idea. Ben

159

started working on the project, but it wasn't quite finished when a severe thunderstorm was building out west. The TV weatherman reported 80 mph winds were headed into their county.

Just after sunset, the dreaded storm hit with a vengeance. Suz and Ben watched helplessly from their bedroom window. Flashes of lightning lit up the garden area. For a while, Ancestry held her own in the driving wind and rain. They were terribly disappointed when they could tell that she was no longer standing. "If the wind broke her stem, she'll die," Suz spoke sadly. She didn't want their project to end this way.

After the storm passed by, they rushed out to their garden. Using a flashlight, Ben examined Ancestry's hardy stem and said with relief, "It's not broken."

"Hold her up straight, and I'll pack wet mud around her base," Suz suggested.

Once that was done, Ben went back in the house to get some string. He tied it around her stem in several places and to the top support of the cage he'd built. Ancestry was proudly standing tall again. "That was a close call!" he emphasized. "If I had put the plastic around the cage like I'd intended, this wouldn't have happened. It would have protected her. I'll do that tomorrow night after work."

The couple checked on Ancestry's progress daily. It was a treat when she yielded some ripe berries. Ben plopped several in his mouth, "Mmm. Those are good. I don't know why you thought I wouldn't like them."

Suz put a tender berry in her mouth, and a rush of seeds memorably burst forth along with an abundance of familiar flavor. Her reaction was the same, "Mmm. Does that ever take me back in time!"

They would have liked to have eaten all the berries she produced, but they had to be wise. Like Mom, Suz carefully saved seeds every time she washed off a few berries. Near the end of the growing season, they let the remaining berries dry up and cling to her stems. They would naturally fall to the ground when it was time. In late October, a killing freeze ended Ancestry's life.

Or had it? The next spring, Suz and Ben discovered tiny berry plants coming up where she had grown. "Ancestry did her job!" Ben exclaimed cheerfully.

The couple was now on a mission to start a real blackberry garden. They transplanted 12 tiny bushes to another location, which had protection from the wind. They left four plants growing in the area where Ancestry had been in case the relocated ones didn't make it.

The blackberries in both areas thrived from flower stage to ripe berries. Then the birds discovered them. They came in to peck away, but Suz and Ben fought back. They hung things around the garden to scare them away. For the most part, it worked. The birds didn't venture into the territory very often.

Ben and Suz had fun eating berries right off the vine and making desserts with them. One of the recipes she made was called blackberry coffee cake. It was similar to the Rivel Kuga her ancestors had made years ago.

Ancestry's journey really didn't begin in Kansas. No, it began over 100 years ago in poor villages in Russia. From 1911 to 1913, four families in Suz's family tree left the Old Country in search of a better life in America. On their immigrant journeys, the Ertles, Gartners (name changed in America to Gertners), Lambrechts and Hochnadels brought with them precious blackberry seeds. It would mean free food for them and a link to their past.

In America, all of their journeys began as lowly laborers in sugar beet fields. Through diligent efforts, they eventually worked their way up to farming on their own. Each of them attentively cared for their beloved schwartzbeeren (blackberries.) They saw the fruit-bearing plants grow in the fields of Russia and in the fields of America. Now, their descendants can look at their legacy and see how blackberries became intertwined into the fields of their lives.

Blackberries grown in 2012 from seed that was originally brought over from Russia by ancestors a century ago. Remarkably, a piece of ancestry was "handed down" through tiny seeds.

Suz enjoyed the fruitful journey she went on during her family tree research. She now realizes that her ancestors nourished two seeds in their lifetimes, which are still living today – faith and blackberries. Both had been "planted" before her eyes all along, but now she sees them in a new light.